VOICES from the DRUG CULTURE

VOICES from the DRUG CULTURE

Harrison Pope, Jr.

BEACON PRESS   BOSTON

Beacon Press books are published under the auspices of the Unitarian Universalist Association

Published simultaneously in Canada by Saunders of Toronto, Ltd.

Printed in the United States of America

Designed by Linda Scovill

For my father,
with much love

CONTENTS

vii

ACKNOWLEDGEMENTS

I began this work as a thesis at Harvard College under the direction of three outstanding tutors. Erik Erikson gave me encouragement and guidance to get started, advice about my field experience, and wise commentary on my initial impressions. Dr. Paul Walters, a psychiatrist experienced with drug users, introduced me to many of the psychoanalytical aspects of drug use. Finally, George W. Goethals supervised my work on the thesis during my senior year. Though he helped me in every way with both my conclusions and my style, he never pressed me to adopt his own techniques or hypotheses. For this independence I am most grateful.

I cannot count the people all over the country who read the original thesis and offered their comments. In particular I want to remember the late Richard Hofstadter, who read the thesis and encouraged me to get it published. His wife, Beatrice, and daughter, Sarah, also offered excellent suggestions. Of the many physicians who read the thesis, Dr. Mark Altschule and Dr. David Lewis were especially helpful. In rewriting the text, I have followed many of their expert comments. For help in the final stages of my work, I am deeply indebted to the entire staff of The Sanctuary in Cambridge, particularly David Bynum, Jeffrey Blum, Judy Smith, and Richard Margolin. Finally, Carol Carlington, Linda Scovill, and Kathy Lawrence helped immeasurably in preparing the final manuscript for publication.

Most of all I thank the hundreds of users I have known, from whom I learned not only about drugs, but about all aspects of life. I hope that a few of them will someday come across this book, where they will recognize themselves, under various pseudonyms, and think back, as I have so often, to old times.

Harrison Pope, Jr.
Roxbury, Massachusetts
May 1971

I. THE SCENE

It was five o'clock in the morning. Maybe seven o'clock. Maybe the sun was shining brightly outside, but there was no way to tell. The single window of the apartment was so dirty that it was almost opaque, and I could barely see the brick wall of another building about ten feet beyond. A smashed windowpane was imperfectly caulked with a towel; during the night, a little cone of very fine snow had formed on the sill beneath it.

The only other light in the room came from a row of candles stuck to the mantlepiece. Most were out, but a few still burned dimly, casting flickering shadows on the walls and ceiling. Little droplets of red, green, and blue wax rolled off the candles to the edge of the mantlepiece and plopped onto the mattresses on the floor. On one mattress was a chessboard, spattered with wax, the pieces set in a half-completed game. As I watched, a fat cockroach scuttled across the board, laboriously climbed to the top of a pawn, peered around, then ran away and vanished in a crack.

The apartment was a single room with an adjoining cubicle that contained a toilet. The door to the cubicle was closed, because the toilet had not been working for the last three days, and the smell had become objectionable. No one had tried to fix it; it was easier to use the toilet in the apartment next door. The whole room had a strong odor of urine, but I had been there too many hours to notice it any longer.

The floor of the room was completely covered with old mattresses except for a small space in the center occupied by a coffee table. On the table were little packets of aluminum foil, large ones containing amphetamine and smaller ones containing DMT deposited on parsley. One was half open, spilling out pure white crystals which glistened in the candlelight. Near it lay several bright orange Thorazine tablets, two green-and-black capsules of Librium, and a group of little home-made capsules, each half-filled with pink powder: crushed up "Owsley tabs" of LSD. Two little brass pipes, still filled with gray lumps of burned hashish, lay amid the pieces of a larger pink glass water pipe that someone had taken apart for cleaning. A teaspoon, its bottom blackened with carbon, still held a few white specks and the remains of a cigarette filter. Next to it, an ashtray, filled with cigarette butts, various kinds of ashes, and little balls of aluminum foil, overflowed onto the table. At the far end of the table, in a glass of milky water, rested a needle with a dropper serving as a syringe. It was used by everyone in the apartment, and it had received one dip in the glass between injections.

Around the sides of the room, so silent that one hardly noticed them at first, sat seven people — five boys and two girls. All were quite wide awake, but none moved or spoke. One boy sat crumpled in a corner, his face hidden in his hands, as though he were trying to expose a minimum of his body surface to the air. A girl lying on the floor held one hand in front of her eyes and meticulously studied her fingers. The others sat along the wall opposite the mantlepiece, staring into the candlelight with motionless expressions, seemingly unconscious of each other's presence.

The only disturbance in the stillness was the faint sound of the little phonograph on the floor, which had been playing continuously for the last sixty hours. Through the crackles and scratches filtered the distant voice of Donovan, soothing and almost mournful. It was the last record of the pile, but no one got up to change it. And so it played the same haunting song, over, and over, and over:

> So begins another Spring
> Green leaves and of berries
> Chiff-chaff eggs are painted by
> Motherbird eating cherries.

I felt totally disconnected from the outside world; the walls of the little room were the borders of the universe. It was hard to believe that my friends at college were sitting around the dormitory, passing the time until they could go to the dining hall, and worrying about final exams. Even the steel-and-glass skyscrapers of central Manhattan, a mere two miles away — aggressive executives and cool secretaries, plush boutiques, pedestrians in jackets and ties, angry cab drivers — all seemed so remote as to be totally unreal. The feeling of unreality persisted long after I returned to my room at college a few days later. Things there seemed so neat and clean, so organized and scheduled, and as I sat in the oak-panelled dining hall, surrounded by dim portraits of illustrious alumni, debating sociology with my friends, I felt uncomfortable, out of place, and a bit of a coward.

That scene on the Lower East Side took place in the winter of 1968. In 1969, when I wrote my college thesis on drug use, I included a description of it, because it was typical of many places that I had seen while living with what were then known as the hippies. I predicted at that time, on the basis of my first-hand experience and everything I knew of psychology and sociology, that the scene was going to spread, that drug use of all forms was going to rise steadily among American youth. But the public did not seem to think so. In the summer of 1969, people were saying that the hippies were passé and that LSD use had passed its peak. Even the media found other topics to arouse audiences. But events began to disturb this complacency, perhaps most dramatically when Woodstock drew 300,000 people. Gradually, all across America, parents and teachers of high school students, junior high school students, and occasionally even fifth and sixth graders, began to discover that things were not as benign as they seemed. The dim apartments and the coffee tables filled with drugs, once clustered in only a few little patches of the country, such as New York, Los Angeles, and San Francisco, were springing up everywhere: in plush Philadelphia suburbs, in North Carolina college communities, in Texas border towns, and in remote parts of the Midwest and West. The wave had spread across both national borders: thirty different batches of LSD were circulating in Vancouver when I was there in the summer of 1970, and thousands of Americans and Canadians were buying them. And, despite numerous federal schemes, even fourteen- and fifteen-year-olds were regularly bringing in tons of marijuana from Mexico.

When asked to rewrite my thesis for publication in late 1970, I began talking with people in the drug world, some old friends and some new. It emerged that even in my rather bold predictions of two years before, I had underestimated the extent to which drug use would spread. The following replies, though they may sound startling, are only a representative sample of a much larger number that I have heard in talking to youths of all ages from more than twenty-five states.*

A 19-year-old boy who graduated from high school in Sacramento, California:

> The scene there was almost as big as it was in San Francisco, because everybody would drive down to the coast, and find out what was going on, and buy stuff and bring it back up. So sure, there was a lot of dope and acid and speed and skag, barbs, and other downs. Not too many people got into skag, but *everybody* smoked grass and lots of people had taken acid a hundred times.

A medical student who had graduated from the same high school in 1965:

> Well, you know, when I was there, there were no drugs at all. Nobody had even heard of drugs for all practical purposes. And then it sort of appeared overnight. As late as 1967 there were practically no

*In most of the quotes in this book, marijuana is called "grass" or "dope," LSD is "acid," amphetamine is "speed" or "ups," heroin is "skag," and depressants in general are called "downs."

drugs there, and then about two years later everybody was doing it.

A college student from Texas:

> You know, my little brother is only 13 years old and he's tripped on acid already. And so have all his friends. They treat it about the way I treated alcohol — they go to the hamburger stand while tripping and go into the house and talk to my mother — Jesus Christ, man it's getting ridiculous! I mean, you know how many times I've taken acid — I have nothing against acid, but in the eighth grade? At the hamburger stand?

A boy from a small city in Iowa:

> I knew personally fifteen kids in my high school class who had taken heroin.

A girl from a town of 4,000 in Idaho:

> Now that sophomores in *my* high school are taking dope and acid, I *know* that the scene has spread all over the country.

An art student just graduated from high school in an affluent Philadelphia suburb:

> In my high school, I'd say that between five and ten percent of the boys and one or two percent of the girls were real heads, people who didn't do much of anything except take LSD and sometimes speed and heroin.

A boy from a prestigious Eastern preparatory school:

> When the student council did a survey in 1968, they found that forty percent of the students and, would you believe, several percent of the faculty, had smoked grass. Since that survey there's absolutely no question that it's been going up. And acid's unquestionably over ten percent, maybe far more.

A college graduate who taught for a year at a smaller co-educational prep school:

I was really amazed at how many of the boys had taken something stronger than dope. They treat LSD so lightly in comparison to the way we thought about it. When I was in college it was a big deal — I planned when I was going to do it about a month in advance and so on. But these guys play football when they're tripping, *football,* and they play better than when they're straight. God knows how they do it.

These quotes all concern teenagers in high school. For those who have dropped out of high school and run away from home, the picture is even more dramatic. An example is this conversation with a drug dealer in Boston who has remained close to the heart of the scene:

"Well you know about how it was for your average runaway kid to score skag on the Common in the summer of 1968. It wasn't as easy as getting grass, maybe, but it wasn't too hard. Well, the difference now is that there's a lot more of it, but the dealing scene is getting a lot riskier. Kids are getting ripped off all the time. Good friend of mine lost five pounds of beautiful dope to some cat with a knife on the street, and he considers that a routine loss. Well, I can't take that sort of scene. That's why I moved out of dealing."

"How much of the ripping off is by kids who need money for heroin?"

"Gee, I don't really know. Part of it is lower class kids who are mixing with the street people in order to hit all the ones who are too stupid to be careful about who they're dealing with. A lot of *them* may be on skag. Then the whole street scene has become a lot heavier — it's a real dog-eat-dog situation now. I mean, a lot of kids need money just for food. So that accounts for some of it. But sure, a lot of the ripping off is caused by stupid kids who get way into skag and suddenly realize they can't get off again."

"How about coke?"

"Well, cocaine still remains the prestige drug. Everybody wants cocaine. And it's still expensive as hell — I've heard of people paying twenty-five dollars for a gram that was lucky to be even thirty percent cocaine. The difference is that two years ago, people were sort of wary about coke. Only a few of them were willing to shoot it. Now *everybody* wants it. They pour out a little pile without worrying too much about the dose and shoot it up. And you know how tricky that stuff is — one guy will get whacked out of his mind on a dose that won't even touch somebody else. A lot of these kids just don't treat coke with proper *respect!*"

A friend of mine, who has known many of the street people in Cambridge during the last year, had this to say:

If I had to summarize in one word what has happened to the street scene in the last two years, it would be "decay." There's no more of the old-time hippies, no more of the "festival of life" thing. It's not so much love any more, but survival. The whole scene has gotten much heavier, more rip offs now, and of course, more downs: barbiturates and heroin and things like that. The street scene is getting to be a tough place for a kid to come to, a dangerous place. For your average sixteen-year-old kid who runs away from home — and there are a lot that young or younger — he's not really prepared to cope with some of the dangers of the scene a lot of the time. I'm not sure that there are many more runaway kids than two years ago, but even if the number hasn't changed, the hassles have gotten a lot bigger.

Drug use among college students has not increased as drastically as at the high school level in the last two years, primarily because it was so high already. Along the East Coast and in California, the amount of college drug use may even have reached the point where it is levelling off, with other regions of the country running a year or two behind.

In order to obtain some hard data on college drug use, I performed a very carefully controlled study on the class of 1969 at a large eastern university (Pope, et al. in preparation). The study was based on a sample of more than 500 students randomly selected from the entire class, with careful measures ensuring the respondents of anonymity. More than 95% of the questionnaires were filled out and returned. Nearly 70% of the boys and 60% of the girls stated that they had used marijuana, more than 20% of the boys and 15% of the girls had used LSD, mescaline, STP, or other "big" hallucinogens, and more than 5% of both girls and boys had used morphine, heroin, or cocaine. They also mentioned amphetamines, barbiturates, laboratory alcohol, bottles of cough syrup, nose drops, amyl nitrate, ether, type cleaner, and cigarettes dipped in after-shave lotion. It was the consensus of practically all the students and faculty at the university that the class of 1970 would produce considerably higher figures than 1969, with 1971 probably about the same as 1970. Most of them felt that the level of drug use at their particular institution was somewhat higher than the national average for major liberal arts universities, but that the gap was closing each year. Their impressions are consistent with my observations and conversations all over the country. On the basis of this, I would estimate that in the class of 1971 at major American universities, a minimum of 12% of the students have used LSD or other big hallucinogens, and 4% of the students have used morphine or heroin. A less guarded and probably more realistic estimate would be 20% for hallucinogens and 10% for opiates. And this does not include students who dropped out of college, for whom the figures are probably higher.

It is difficult to quantify more exactly the extent of drug use among America's youth, but the number that has used some drug *beyond* marijuana is definitely into the millions, possibly as high as three million, and still growing. Drug use is spreading from its old urban centers to communities that have never seen it before. It is reaching down to younger and younger age groups. Bigger drugs are being used: marijuana has grown commonplace, LSD is rapidly becoming so, and amphetamine, cocaine, and heroin use have increased tremendously. Drug use and drug dealing are overlapping more and more with violent crime, organized and otherwise: for those who leave home, the street scene in general is becoming increasingly dangerous. And perhaps the most striking change is that bigger drugs are becoming ordinary, even trivial. Once respected as a deep philosophical and psychological journey, for some people LSD has become something to see colors with, to play football with, to take before going to the hamburger stand. And even drugs as dangerous as cocaine and heroin have become ordinary in places where they would have been shunned two years, a year, or even months ago.

How did the scene get so big, and why is it still growing? No one seems to possess enough of an overview to answer this question. Parents throw up their hands and say that kids have it too easy nowadays, or that it must be the result of a malicious minority, or that it is all exaggerated by the newspapers. The drug users themselves are aware that it is not due to a minority and not exaggerated, but they too tend to oversimplify its origins; to most of them it seems like "just fun" or something that all of their friends were doing. Journalists describe its aspects but fail to probe its psychological and sociological background; academicians offer attractive theories, but are too "straight" to join the subculture and collect reliable data to support them. This book attempts to span these points of view. Although it makes use of the psychological, sociological, and pharmacological literature, as well as the musical "literature" of rock songs, it is based primarily on my own participant observation with a diverse group of more than two thousand drug users across the country. Most of the users were of high school or college age, but they were not necessarily attending school. They ranged in socioeconomic background from lower-middle class to upper class. Some used only marijuana, but most also used LSD and other hallucinogens, amphetamines and opiates. A few used amphetamines or heroin exclusively. Finally, since boys far outnumbered girls in the street scene and among heavy users, the group contained more than twice as many boys as girls, a fact reflected in the emphasis of some chapters. The Appendix contains the full details of my technique and the methods used to ensure the accuracy of my findings.

All descriptions of drug use and drug users in this book, unless otherwise indicated, are based specifically on my personal experience with them. From this foundation in observation, and from my training in psychology, sociology, and medicine, I have tried to construct a more systematic and comprehensive explanation of the origins of drug use than has been previously available to the public. Unlike most earlier studies, it is not based on speculation or clinical experience, but on actual involvement with the drug subculture. Though these users were subjects for a study, they were, above all, my contemporaries and friends. I was as much a participant as an observer.

II. LAUREN

When I met him two years ago, Lauren was nineteen years old, a tall, lean boy who always wore old blue jeans and a faded flannel shirt. He was the oldest of three children in a well-to-do Anglo-Saxon family, Easter-Sunday Protestants, in a suburban town about fifteen miles from Boston. His father was a lawyer in a large Boston firm, a busy man who spent nine hours a day at the office and two more commuting in and out of the city. Lauren was not quite sure what his father did in his work; it had something to do with corporations and taxes, it was specialized and complex, and it paid well. Lauren felt that he did not really know his father; he had trouble describing him to me.

> Well, he was sort of a distant man, sort of quiet. Basically I think he was just not capable of much emotion. He liked to be alone in his house. He was uncomfortable about going to parties. It always used to make my mother mad because she was just the opposite. She could have migraines and she'd still want to go to a party. Dad just wasn't a very friendly man — I mean he never showed much warmth toward

me or my mother.... You know something freaky? It's really hard to imagine that he ever had sex with my mother. Well, I exist, so I suppose he must have. Maybe my mother had a secret lover instead.

He laughed and shook his head to indicate the remoteness of that possibility.

"Don't get me wrong, Dad was a perfectly nice man, but he was politically conservative, and really straight, and, well, he was just wrapped up in the old money and suburbia possession bag, you know, sort of a boring life, just — boring."

"So your mother got bored with him and found a secret lover?"

"Perhaps she should have, but it wouldn't even have occurred to her."

"What was she like?"

"She was much warmer and more emotional than my father, and she didn't criticize me and belittle me. She was sort of an obsessive-compulsive, meticulously neat and organized person. She was also really ambitious for me. She made me take piano lessons for six years. I was in high school before I came to my senses and told her to fuck off."

Lauren had attended the excellent high school in his home town, and he got A's and B's with little effort. He never took any interest in his courses or in sports, but he had a lot of friends.

"What did you do with them?" I asked.

"Well, there wasn't much to do. We weren't old enough to drive then. We went to movies sometimes, but that got to be a drag. We went — hell, we didn't really have anything to do. We all lusted after getting cars and motorcycles, and when we got them, it only made it so we could go nowhere faster."

"Did you do much with girls?"

"I started seeing chicks when I was about sixteen, I guess, but I never got into the stupid dating thing that the straighter kids did. It was ridiculous, it was a real down. I first made it with a chick when I was seventeen. She was nice — we saw a lot of each other before I graduated."

Marijuana hit Lauren's high school when he was a junior:

"I first learned about it when I found out that some of the other kids I knew were getting it from their older brothers, or from Boston. Somebody knew a dealer who had kilograms of really good stuff. And we all got into it. It was like about six months between the time nobody took dope and everybody was smoking."

"Why did everybody go for it so fast?"

"Same reason that I did. Boredom. It really was something to do for a change. You know what I think of? There was this teacher I had in my senior year who always used to go on about how the kids were smoking grass because they didn't want to confront life and their responsibilities and their problems and so on. You know, the old 'drugs for escape' thing that most of the adults believe. Shit, man, there *wasn't* any life to confront in that town! The whole place was a drag. The reason we got into dope was exactly the opposite of what he thought."

"Any other reasons?"

"Well, also because everybody else was doing it. You know, it was the thing to do. All the college kids were doing it, and the media were making a big thing out of it. Yeah, especially the media — I think that that influenced a lot of kids to get into drugs."

"When did you get into acid?"

"That was in my senior year. Things had really changed a lot by the time I graduated from high school. By that time lots of ninth graders were doing dope and some were doing acid. I just got into acid because, well sort of like Mount Everest, because it was there. And of course I'd seen all these things on TV and had these programs in school where they tell you that dope is dangerous and you'll freak out and so on. And so when I found out how much they had lied about dope, I figured they probably were lying about acid, too, which they were."

"How many times have you taken acid since then?"

"Oh, God, I have no idea how many times, but it's been a lot. Acid is the sort of thing that's impossible to take only once. I just can't imagine anybody taking it only once. It's like peanuts."

"Peanuts?"

"Well, not really, but you know what I mean. After you've had a taste of it you just have to go back and see more. It's the exact opposite of boredom. I've had all kinds of experiences on acid — joy, sadness, love, hate, terror, you name it, but I sure as hell have *never* been bored."

"How much did your parents know?"

"Well, they never really wanted to believe I was into drugs, and anyway they couldn't tell. It even got so that my brother and I would get stoned and go to dinner. They never noticed a thing. Except that I used to spill things all the time when I ate stoned. You know how you get really hungry on dope and you shove a big piece of roast beef in your mouth, and gravy dribbles all over your face. I used to have my napkin completely covered with gravy by the end of the meal, and olive pits on the floor, and whipped cream on my shirt, feeling just great, and my mother would look over at me and say 'Oh, Lauren, can't you be neater than that?' And then she'd go on about how she brought me up better than that and my brother and I would look at each other and try to keep from laughing."

"What about when you told them you weren't going to college?"

"That was the first thing that really shook them up, I think. My mother cried and said she had failed and my father was just stony and silent. I told them that I'd probably go to college eventually, but that I needed another kind of education. I needed to see the rest of the world. That summer I hitchhiked to California and had a really good time. I was going to live out there, you know, but I started having bad vibes with the people I was out there with, so I went to Texas — to Austin — where I've got a friend in college. They had a lot of peyote down there and we tripped on that. God, it was beautiful stuff. I didn't even get sick to my stomach. Then I came back to Boston and spent the winter with six other people in an apartment in Brighton. That was sort of a bad scene — we shot up skag and shot up coke and shot up speed. But especially we did acid. We got our hi-fi system and a lot of acid ripped off last March, and we almost got busted in May and generally it was a bad scene. I made some money selling acid and dope back at my high school, and I bought a car, and I and another guy drove down to Mexico and bought fifty pounds of grass way down in Oaxaca and drove it back through Tijuana in another guy's car during the Saturday night rush. We've still got a bunch of that left and it's *dynamite*, man. Want to try some?"

"What are you going to do this winter?"

"I'm going back to Texas. I'm not going to spend another winter in this polluted city. I'm going to stay with Bill in Austin for a while and then figure out where to go from there. I'm getting a little tired of drugs — I'm getting more into a religious thing now. I think I might go out to the mountains in western Texas and just spend a month or two alone — you know, live off the land, and meditate, maybe fast for a few days and then take some peyote. I want to get away from people. Also I've been starting to have a few hassles with my parents and I want to get out of this goddamned city."

I think that most Americans have known at least one boy like Lauren — a seemingly ordinary boy from a nice, stable family, from a nice high school in an ordinary community, who abruptly left everything behind and went to the city to take drugs — the sort of boy about whom the neighbors remark that "no one would have guessed."

But one could have guessed, for Lauren's story has many elements which I have heard over and over again from drug users all over the country. His story is an introduction to these elements, a reminder that they cannot be completely dissected out, that they fit in various ways into a whole life style: the thoughts, feelings and actions of a real person.

III. BOREDOM AND FUN

Something Inside That Was Always Denied

What is the single most important reason why middle class American youths take drugs? The answer is simple: for fun. This might seem too obvious to merit further discussion, but in fact an extraordinary number of people, both old and young, simply do not comprehend it. I encounter this whenever I talk about drugs, among high school teachers, college professors, doctors, lawyers, policemen, parents, and even students; their misunderstanding is regularly revealed in one question: "But why do the kids *need* to take drugs?"

Marijuana or LSD use is very rarely the compulsive satisfaction of an acute need. Practically all users perceive taking these drugs as mere enjoyment. The user feels no more *need* to take hallucinogens than another person feels a need to drive a sports car. Both are activities which promise to be pleasurable, albeit risky. Drug use, like driving sports cars, may of course reflect more subtle, unconscious "psychological" needs, but its primary attraction is fun.

The reader who is surprised or angered by such an analogy may find that he is making three questionable assumptions. The first is that drug use is such a formidable and frightening thing that no one would try it unless he needed it badly. This is simply wrong. In most high schools and colleges, not to mention on the streets, a potential user can observe his peers going to movies, driving cars, talking with their parents, playing sports, and even passing exams under the influence of drugs. He may witness a "bad trip," but the vast majority of users he sees will be enjoying themselves. When he ultimately decides to try drugs, he will think in terms of a potentially enjoyable pastime, or a fascinating, even important experience, but hardly the satisfaction of a desperate need.

The second assumption is that all illegal drugs are similar to alcohol, nicotine, and caffeine. But they differ in an important respect: America's three legal mind-altering chemicals are rarely used for sheer enjoyment alone, but to cope with environmental stresses. We take alcohol and nicotine to relax at a party, and coffee to wake up the next morning. Everyone has heard, "I need a drink!" or "I need a cigarette." Illicit drugs (particularly amphetamines and depressants) *may* also be used to cope with the environment, but most youths take them for the enjoyment of the "high" alone. There is nothing particularly entertaining about an alcohol or caffeine high by itself, but the LSD high is a fascinating flow of images and hallucinations, enjoyable in its own right. Even most initial amphetamine or heroin use is primarily for enjoyment of the effects themselves.

The third assumption behind the "need" question is that one must do everything for a purpose, that no one would want to do something just for fun. This stems from the work ethic: the idea that pleasure for its own sake is wrong. Why should someone deliberately go out and do something with his time which he knows is neither useful nor contributing to his future if not to satisfy a need? One reply to this is that users frequently do take drugs with constructive intent, as described in the next chapter. But more often they are hardly influenced by any work ethic; they have no qualms about trying something just for kicks, admitting that they do not need it for any useful purpose.

Some adults are so stubborn in this last assumption that they do not even concede that drug use is enjoyable. "They act as though they're having fun, but they aren't really having fun, are they?" a woman once confided to me. This is absurd. For most of the thousands of drug experiences that I have closely observed, users *are* having fun; to deny this is to forfeit any chance of understanding drug use.

But people who ask the "need" question are not always so naive, for most do realize that drug use is pleasurable and that it is rarely a response to an acute, specific need. The deeper question is more reasonable and difficult: Why, given many possible legal activities that are fun, does a youth choose to try drugs instead? Why do drugs become the *primary* source of fun?

The answer to this question begins with boredom. Like Lauren, drug users usually first mention boredom when asked why they began. But though the feeling is very real and very powerful — that is obvious in almost every case — they have trouble in verbalizing its sources, a problem which often irritates parents who have asked their children to explain just what is wrong. A boy once told me:

> My folks said, "What do you mean you have nothing to do? You have school, and you might be on the basketball team, and you have lots of books and your own TV set, and we let you use the car all the time." They went on and on like that, giving me five hundred irrefutable reasons why there must be something wrong with me if I was bored. And then I remember my mother saying, "Maybe you should see a psychiatrist. Don't you think that if you talked to a psychiatrist a couple of times, it would help you out?" That was typical of their reasoning, you know. They'd given me the car and bought me the TV set, so now they were going to buy me a psychiatrist to put me back in shape again. How can you talk to people like that? How can you possibly explain to them that until drugs came along, there was nothing in this dump that was really, that was really, fun?

This gulf between the perspective of the user and that of his parents is brought out in the old Beatles song, "She's Leaving Home," in which a girl leaves home to try to find:

> Something inside
> That was always denied
> For so many years.

A moment later in the song, her parents sing:

> We gave her everything money could buy.

And:

> What did we do that was wrong?
> We didn't know it was wrong.
> Fun is the one thing that money can't buy.

The last line captures the view of most drug users: the things that money can buy may be momentarily entertaining, but ultimately they are superficial, joyless, lonely, and dull. This is hard for some parents to accept, since they, as the Beatles put it, have "sacrificed most of their lives" for such things. And even if these parents sometimes feel that the accoutrements of affluence really are boring, they are unlikely to admit this to their children.

Brown Shoes Don't Make It

The words of actual users describe these feelings better than any number of abstractions. The first is a girl from Maryland named Paula:

> My mother wanted me to take riding lessons or to go out and do something with the other girls at the high school. I don't know what she wanted me to do with them. Talk about our shampoos maybe. Or how we were choosing a college where we could get married off fast to some eligible boy. She wanted me to go out on dates with these dumb, well-behaved kids that she approved of. Go to a movie, make out in the car, go get a hamburger. Who the hell does she think I am? Work hard in school so you can get into a good college, go to a good college so you can marry an ambitious nurd who will sell insurance and buy you a nice house in the suburbs so you can wash dishes and buy furniture and play bridge with the girls on alternate Tuesdays, so that when you've done this for

fifty years and you die, everybody will say "She was nice" or something like that. Jesus Christ, I can't take any more of her shit. Isn't it normal to want to make love? Isn't it normal to want to have a little adventure? A little excitement for a change? Taking acid is a fuck of a lot *more* normal than sitting around and doing nothing.

Actually Paula uses four-letter words less frequently than a number of her classmates in high school. And yet her mother, whom I have met, has never heard them from her daughter, and would deny that Paula could even have said this. If the two of them differ so much on vocabulary, one shudders to think how irreconcilable are their ideas.

Paula eventually dropped out of high school, as did this boy, an only child, from Rhode Island:

In the summers my family used to go to the beach where we had this summer cottage. All my parents wanted was to be alone and do nothing. They'd sit around the house and work on home improvements or drink, and I would go swimming. And after the first day of swimming, it got to be a real bummer. There just wasn't anything to do, except go around and look for the action, which never existed anyway. And then in the summer after ninth grade, some of my friends down there got some dope, and we would turn on down on the beach at night while my parents were drinking back at home. A couple of times we even smoked in the cottage upstairs from them, but of course they were too smashed to notice anything strange. Those times were really beautiful. There was a real sense of a bond between the kids there, a real sense of fraternity — it was beautiful.

Some of the older and more intellectual users I have known tried to specify more precisely what is wrong. One, a close friend at a western medical school, a former user of LSD, mescaline, DMT, amphetamine, cocaine, opium, and heroin, who, incidentally, graduated *summa cum laude* from Yale, explained:

Within three months after I came to medical school, I had seen a baby get born, and all kinds of people ill, and an old man die from a cerebral hemorrhage. I had never seen a birth or death before, and it made quite an impression on me. In America, nobody ever sees that. It's "Grandpa has gone on a long trip," and the stork bringing the babies, and the meat all cut and attractively packaged at the supermarket. In other societies, every five-year-old has seen birth and death, and his parents screwing, and so on. But everything's so sterile in a super-civilized society like this one. When I think about it, that's one of the reasons I took LSD. I wanted to have a real gut-level experience, to really cut through all my acculturation and look at the heart of life.

A Harvard sociology major, a political activist, who takes LSD once a month said:

One of the things that really disgusts me about this country is the way people remove themselves from real situations and real feelings. Like people watch a TV show on poverty, which wraps up the whole situation into ninety minutes, minus fifteen of commercials. Then they've "done their duty" and gotten informed, and that's all they ever see of it. No wonder life is boring. They keep themselves apart from everything real.

A boy who left the University of Texas after one semester:

Sometimes I wonder why my parents aren't especially bored. I think maybe they are, but they don't dare to try to do anything about it. They lead lives of quiet desperation.

Of course, many parents really do not lead such boring lives as their children imagine. Many genuinely prefer peace and security to an overabundance of excitement or action, though they might not have when they were twenty. But there is more "quiet desperation" to be found than most are willing to admit. The Mothers of Invention have this in mind in their brilliant song, "Brown Shoes Don't Make It," in which they compare the empty life of a middle-aged businessman —

His wife's attending an orchid show.
She's tried for a week to get him to go.

— with his fantasy world:

> While in the bed, his teenage queen
> Is rocking and rolling and acting obscene.

Many users perceive the older generation in much the same way as the Mothers do.

Eating Dinner by the Pool

A moment later in "Brown Shoes," in a phrase dripping with sarcasm, the Mothers focus upon another gripe of drug users:

> Eating dinner by the pool
> I'm so glad I finished school.

Is this the only purpose of school, to teach students how to get rich and live in comfort? Hopefully not, but after their high school and college experiences many drug users think so. "I knew more than my teachers," a girl on the Lower East Side in Manhattan once told me. "I dropped out of high school because there was nothing they could teach me that was worth learning." Is such a statement arrogant and defensive? In part, perhaps, but then how much does Miss Smith know about sex, about love, about the dark recesses of the mind? Has she ever talked with a wino in the South End, or been down and out with no place to sleep, or can she recognize that Mr. Quincey, the history teacher, is obviously gay? Of course Miss Smith may know some of these things, but one would never guess from her classes that she knows, or approves of, anything but English. The stultifying effects of most public schools make it difficult for her to relate image and metaphor in *Silas Marner* to the issues of the contemporary scene.

The complaints are similar even among students in schools with very high academic standards, as suggested by this boy from a famous preparatory school:

> The place was an incredible drag. It was a complete ivory tower. Many of the teachers acted like poverty and racism and the war didn't even exist. On certain days, also, you weren't allowed to go into town because on those days the girls' school nearby let *their* students go into town. What could be more

anti-educational than separating the sexes like that? I mean, getting to meet girls at that age is a much more important part of really learning about the world than courses in academics. Also I wanted to take courses on film, but they only had one stupid course on it, where we got to shoot about two rolls of super-eight apiece. They seemed to work on the philosophy that the only way to keep us out of trouble was to give us enough homework so that we didn't have time to get into trouble. Also you had to have your lights out and be in bed by 10:30. They treated us like little children in every way. It was really belittling. Oh yeah, we had to go to church every Sunday. That made me into an atheist, of course.

These are common themes in the accounts of high school students, including some who have not dropped out and not taken drugs: too much restriction, childish rules, emphasis on competition, and most of all, the irrelevance of academic material to what John Phillips called "the real business of living." Are these students complaining merely because they could not perform very well in academic work? This would not be consistent with my observations: many of the users stated that they had been in the upper half of their classes. Also, in my study of college users, already cited, even the heaviest users obtained the same grades as non-users.

College education introduces some different problems, which are described by a close friend named Eliot, a high-ranking student who dropped out of Harvard:

Well, first I majored in math, but it was terrible. I didn't see what writing a thesis about numbers had to do with anything real. Then I tried German literature for awhile, but it required that I spend a great deal of time on the language, and reading obscure criticisms of equally obscure sixteenth century works. Then it was philosophy. But the required course in symbolic logic was so obnoxious that I couldn't stand it. It was completely irrelevant to the areas of philosophy that interested me. This university "sets the intellectual pace of the free world," and it doesn't have any courses to speak of in Eastern philosophies! In every field, you quickly find yourself forced into nitpicking and technicalities. Physics deals with subatomic particles, biology with cellular ultrastructure, psychology with pigeons pecking keys, philosophy with symbolic logic. Every field has been devastated by our technocracy. It's not entirely the fault of the college, I admit, but a result of the information explosion: you have to spend years in a pinpoint field to reach the frontiers of knowledge. Just as technology has deprived the factory worker of making a finished product, we are victimized by the mass production of ideas.

And with it comes the insistence on competition. Constantly reading the journals and books to keep up with the other guy, worrying about getting a hot-shot professor to advise your thesis. I think, in retrospect, that that is why I developed an interest in Haitian history — it was a tiny, esoteric field, not yet devastated by the expanding wave of the information explosion. To be an absolute expert on Haitian history gave me a little sense of accomplishment, a momentary relief from the routine of courses. Similarly, I think that was one of the things that got me into LSD — it promised an entirely new kind of intellectual vision, a vast, unexplored field never contaminated by the technical approach of the West.

Now, as you know I'm taking a year off. I may never come back. I want to find some excitement, something non-trivial to use my mind on, something non-competitive, something really *adventurous* to break me from my overwhelming feelings of apathy. I've been thinking of going to the Amazon and taking yage with the natives. Yage is supposed to make LSD or even psilocybin seem like child's play by comparison.

There is little I can add to this account, save to point out that Eliot, like many others, was not bored with the intellectual work or frightened by the competition because he was a poor student. It is a year and one-half since he dropped out, and he has not returned. I think he is now in Mexico City.

Such complaints about school, from the simplest to the most intellectual, are hardly new. Students have always complained about school. But modern American students are singularly disturbed by its irrelevance and by its insensibility to both social and personal problems. The efforts of students to change the political aspects of their situation are history, but few have even dreamed of reforming the more subtle, personal irrelevance of school, of making it into a relief from, rather than another source of apathy. The alternatives for many, particularly at the high school level, may be to take advantage of the greater availability of marijuana and LSD to shake boredom, or to look for excitement by dropping out of school entirely, rather than to try to revolutionize the administration.

Competitive and achievement-oriented parents are angered by their children's dissatisfaction with school. They ask: "How are kids going to get anywhere if they want to spend half their school time studying non-academic material? They are going to be sorry when they get out and look for a job. They should be thankful for the golden opportunity they are being given by going to a good school or college." Most adults believe strongly in these things, but sometimes they have doubts which they must suppress. As Philip Slater has aptly put it in his book, *Pursuit of Loneliness* (Slater 1970), the fathers who "philosophize over the back fence with complete sincerity about their 'dog-eat-dog world' and what-is-it-all-for and you-can't-take-it-with-you and success-doesn't-make-you-happy-it-just-gives-you-ulcers-and-a-heart-condition" get enraged when their children start taking such ideas seriously and waste their opportunity in school. Slater goes on to say:

> Indeed, the degree of rage is, up to a point, a function of the degree of sincerity: if an individual did not feel these things he would not have to fight them so vigorously. The peculiarly exaggerated hostility that hippies tend to arouse suggests that the life they strive for is highly seductive to middle-class Americans. (p. 7)

Many users perceive their parents' doubts; in response to the "golden opportunity" argument, they ask, "opportunity for what?" They think of the ulcers rather than the success. A more colorful expression of the same thing is from an LSD user named Tony:

> A Suzuki is a kind of dog that is faster and smarter than a greyhound. You know why they don't race

them instead of greyhounds? Because when they had the mechanical rabbit going around the track, one of the Suzukis stopped running and sat down to wait for the rabbit to come around to him! That's why I dropped out of college — the competition was pointless.

Tony has returned to college for the same reason that most of the other dropouts have: he has not discovered anything enjoyable about a college education, but his experience in the outside world has shown him that acquiring a degree, though a bore, does expedite the hassles of earning a living. Thus Tony's Suzuki theory (or, if you will, the "Lilies of the Field" theory) did not prove entirely accurate. College, he would concede, is an opportunity, but hardly a golden one. Tony is doing the minimum amount of studying necessary to pass, and to keep himself occupied, he plays poker, looks for girls, and continues to use hallucinogens and amphetamines at least once a week.

Alienation

This is the prelude to drug use: a feeling of boredom rather than need. To potential users, life is unexciting, lacking in action, too much like the dull lives of their parents. Cars, motorcycles, movies, television, sports, and other "acceptable" activities promise only transitory and inadequate amusement. They feel deprived of real involvement, of gut-level experiences. They see no opportunities for commitment, no source of meaning. In particular, school is irrelevant and therefore dull, restrictions too severe, competition overemphasized. In every story from Lauren's to Tony's, apathy is the result of a rejection of basic values in American culture. Usually it is not a violent rejection, though it may contain elements of anger; it is more a gradual process of dropping out. Most importantly, it is an emotional rather than intellectual rejection; drug users rarely try to reason it out. They know that they feel bored, and they find excitement in drugs: it is as simple as that. Drug use begins with a loss of interest in the American way of life.

Sociologists call this loss of interest alienation. As will be seen in the reference notes, much has been written about it, most notably Kenneth Keniston's *The Uncommitted* (Keniston 1960). The reader who wishes to pursue in more detail the origins and characteristics of alienated youths should read this book.

Practically all of the drug users in this country began as alienated youths. Some derive a partial sense of identity from the drug subculture itself, but in all other respects most were still fundamentally alienated at the time that I knew them. Most do not reach the crystallized extreme of alienation described in *The Uncommitted;* they are more optimistic, and though equally alienated from American society, they are not as alienated from their peers as Keniston's subjects. Even the minimal, fluid commitment required by the drug subculture is strong enough to "pinch" a totally alienated youth; he must have some residual faith in his peers, however completely he rejects his elders and the Establishment, in order to join the drug world.

Drug users can be defined as alienated primarily because they show the same pattern of rejection of American society and, up to the point of drug use, the same life style as Keniston's group. For instance, compare Keniston's story of Inburn (p. 23) with that of Lauren in the previous chapter. With a few corrections for the decade that separated them (for example, when Inburn was in college, LSD was not available), the similarity is striking.

Secondly, drug users share all of the "sociological" characteristics of the alienated group as a whole: they are young, the majority of them boys from middle- to upper-class families (with a recent increase in working-class youths), most of them urban and suburban, in the United States and a few other technologically advanced societies. The origins of alienation have been discussed in detail in the literature; my participant observation has little to add to this sociological and historical perspective. The rest of this book covers the second part of the question: given alienation, how does a youth get into drug use?

Before continuing with this question, two details are worth mentioning. First, drug use in the lower socioeconomic classes is a different phenomenon from the drug use described here. It involves more "downs" and less LSD, it is motivated by forces different from Keniston's alienation, and it is chronic: drug use in the lower income groups has not shown such an abrupt increase in the last few years. This is not to say that it is unimportant, or irrelevant to the group in this book, for lower-class drug users certainly do mix with the middle- and upper-class ones. But the acute situation described here begins in the working class and extends to the very top of the upper class in America, reaching its peak in the middle and upper-middle classes.

Second, alienation does not necessarily lead to drug use. It may lead to nothing in particular (as in many of Keniston's subjects), or it may lead to some form of activism: anti-war, preservation of the environment, women's liberation, and so forth. When activism is a response to alienation, it serves as an intellectualization of personal alienation and a shield against the vacuum of uncommitment: the very intensity of involvement is a measure of the emptiness which lies outside. Or it serves, as drug use sometimes does, as a focus for non-specific anger: the issue at hand becomes unimportant and it is only the violence of the response that counts. This is not to say that all activism arises in this way, nor that it would always be unjustified even if it did. It is simply to point out that although activism may at first appear diametrically opposed to the withdrawal symbolized by drug use, some of it reduces to the same feelings.

The Search for Sentience

The appropriateness of applying the alienation concept to drug use is demonstrated in one of users' responses to boredom; a search for new feelings and new awareness. Keniston describes this for the general case of alienation as follows:

> The more passive form of the cult of the present is the *search for sentience,* and it is this search that characterizes the alienated. Here the self is defined not by action, but by perception; and meaning is created by heightened receptivity and openness. Experience is defined as subtlety, sensitivity, and awareness: the purpose of existence is not to alter the world so as to create new experiences, but to alter the self so as to receive new perceptions from what is already there. (p. 181)

This was written when hallucinogens were practically unknown in this country, yet one can hear the word "LSD" in every line: its effects answer perfectly to the desire for new perceptions and awareness. If this is not obvious, compare the following description from a girl in Cambridge, Massachusetts:

> It's a drag to do acid and just sit in a room and listen to music. I like to go out and walk around. Like last week I walked down to the Square, and it was amazing all the things I could see that I hadn't looked at before. Like the opals on display at the jeweller's — one would look at you angrily and one would beam at you and one would stare at you with an icy stare. And then all the trivial little things that you usually ignore — the oil in the puddles on the street, and the distorted reflections in store windows, and the shiny magazines outside the newsstand on the island. And most of all, all the depths of expression on the faces of all the people, people with faces that are trying to look neutral, but are actually screaming their fears and their hopes and their lusts. There's just so much to see.

This sensation of heightened sensitivity, of "altering the self so as to receive new perceptions from what is already there," is a famous effect of the hallucinogens and, in more dilute form, even of marijuana (which has very different effects from the "big" hallucinogens). Many people who have used hallucinogens, most notably Aldous Huxley, have conjectured that this occurs because hallucinogens knock out the brain's usual mechanisms for censoring "trivial" input in the interest of efficiency (Huxley 1954). One would be paralyzed if he were continually distracted by the texture of a door, the color of a book, the sound of rain. But after taking a hallucinogen, one feels like a child, constantly "turned on" by little stimuli, and it is impossible to get bored. This is one reason that some hallucinogen users feel a need to "program" their trips — they might otherwise spend hours entranced with different aspects of bookcase, a neon sign, or a potted plant.

How does LSD interfere with the "censorship" function of the ego? It may block nerve synapses, but a more colorful theory is that it interferes with carbohydrate metabolism in the brain and starves the ego into submission. With big doses of hallucinogens, when the censor is totally starved, comes the ultimate experience of heightened sensitivity: a complete dissolution of the boundaries between self and object, a unity with the cosmos.

The Fusion Experience

In the following sentences from Keniston's description of the alienated, he again almost breathes the word "LSD":

> At root, probably the most powerful unconscious motivation in many of these young men is their desire to merge, to fuse with, to lose themselves in some embracing person, fantasy or group. This *fantasy of mystical fusion* involves the unconscious desire to lose all selfhood in some undifferentiated state with another or with nature, to be totally embraced and to embrace totally. (p. 190)

A college student named Henry was one of many friends who actually experienced the state of fusion on LSD:

> It was the second time I had done acid. The first time was on two hundred mikes or so. It was nice but nothing really spectacular. The second time I took seven or eight hundred mikes — I figured I'd really get a taste of what it was like. Within about twenty minutes I could begin to feel the acid on the top of my spine, and a very subtle tingling in my fingertips. In an hour I was totally zonked and still going up. Every object in the room was moving around — it was wild. Then some guy suggested that we should go swimming in the Adams House pool. So we got the key and went in and God, what an experience! I dived into the water and it just came up and embraced my whole body with this wonderful, sexual feeling. And as I swam, the lights sparkled on the water around my hands, and suddenly I was swimming through a sea of rubies and diamonds and emeralds. And then, a few minutes later, I took a deep breath, and dived underwater, clutched my arms around my knees and hung there, just hung there for centuries and centuries, I mean literally centuries,

with no light and no sound except the distant humming of the pump that keeps the pool full.

It's absolutely futile to attempt to describe in English what that moment felt like. There was no boundary between me and the world. I was everything and everything was me. I had gone back in time — back into the womb, and back before I was even a single cell, when the atoms from which I was made were spread all over the universe. It sounds like a bunch of empty phrases, because it's absolutely impossible to describe to someone who hasn't been there. It was just pure experience, man! Pure, unadulterated experience!

Drug users seek this state of fusion in other ways as well — interpersonally, for example, in their concepts of a perfect relationship and in their often detailed fantasies of an "ideal commune." Sometimes they try LSD as a medicine for dissolving barriers between each other and hastening this. But more often, they use LSD as a source of unadulterated fusion in itself. No other drug, with the possible exception of a couple of the more esoteric hallucinogens, can produce an experience anything like it. If a high school student is aware of this (as many are) and feeling rather bored of an evening, what will he do? He can watch TV, go for a ride with his friends, study math, take a date to the hamburger stand, or for the five-second effort of swallowing two tablets, he might have Henry's experience in the pool.

This is the beginning — boredom and fun are the first feelings described by most drug users. Boredom ranges from mild disenchantment with home and school to the apathy of classical alienation: a complete rejection of American culture, and a life style of uncommitment. Drugs may be fun only in that they appeal to curiosity or to a desire for adventure. But to the more alienated users, drugs become much more intriguing, a source of sentience and fusion, an exciting and meaningful release from the dullness of uncommitment.

IV. THE SHELTERED LIFE

Mother's Boy

At this point the reader may object that I have painted too rosy a picture of LSD. It would indeed be an appealing alternative to boredom if one could always have fascinating walks through the city or cosmic revelations in a swimming pool. But what about the "bad trips," the frightening hallucinations, the suicides, the reports of chromosome damage, the psychoses? What about the dangers of amphetamines and heroin? The answer to this, paradoxically, is that the dangers of LSD and other drugs have even more appeal than their pleasures. This is especially true for boys, who far outnumber girls among heavy users. How does this happen? It begins with a number of themes in the family background of alienated boys in general and of male drug users in particular.

First, many users describe a particular type of relationship with their mothers — a sense of being too close to her, too much under her control, too sheltered and not allowed to grow up completely. This is illustrated in Lauren's story, which is interesting for its sexual overtones. He seemed to feel that he had separated his mother from his father, and perhaps, on some level of his unconscious, he fantasized himself as the "secret lover" in his account. As a matter of fact, since Lauren knew quite a bit about Freud, I once asked him directly what he thought of that hypothesis. He did not quite buy it, but he recalled, with a tinge of anger, that his mother had no hesitations about being nude in his presence, even when he was fifteen or sixteen years old.

Of course I did not interrogate every drug user about his mother, but when the subject came up, the accounts showed marked similarities. One such account is from a boy who dropped out of his first semester at the University of Chicago, who is now a heavy user of amphetamines and heroin:

> My old lady spent a lot of her time with me. She didn't have much else to do, I guess, except play bridge two afternoons a week. She never physically punished me; she would just act hurt when I didn't accomplish something that she wanted. That technique used to make me feel guilty, but when I got older it started really to piss me off.

A 16-year-old from New Jersey:

> She's a nice lady — very docile, completely unliberated. I sort of liked her until she started getting in my way and trying to control me.

A boy in a prep school in Massachusetts:

> My mother got divorced from my father when I was three or four, and I lived alone with her for about five years in our apartment on Park Avenue. I had a very close bond with her then, and it continued to some extent even after my stepfather moved in. She was the one who turned me on to drugs, you know. She used to give me tranquilizers and alcohol even when I was fairly young.

Another common theme in the accounts of drug users is a distant father figure, as in the last account above and in Lauren's story. To be sure, the majority of American fathers spend many hours away from home at their jobs, but users with whom I talked described fathers who were more emotionally distant than average. A typical account of this is from a drug user in Bangor, Maine, named Cory:

> My father was a doctor. He saw the whole world through a microscope and listened to it through a stethoscope. I never had any real communication with him, and I don't think my mother had much, either. I remember when I was in prep school and I made it with a girl for the first time, I told him about it in a letter, just to see if it would break through his shell. He wrote back and had the audacity to say that I was 'sick' for doing it. Sick! And then he never talked about it again. That's one of the few times I ever had any communication with him at all.

The boy from Texas, already quoted, whose 13-year-old brother also takes LSD:

> My old man was so unemotional that it was impossible to really get anything out of him. I think he's really afraid to talk about anything important with me. My mother was the only one I ever talked about sex with, for instance.

Well over half of the users I met described some degree of this background: an intimate, dominating mother and a distant, unemotional father. As will be seen in the reference notes, this family pattern has been described in great detail in the literature of alienation and that of psychoanalysis. The pattern is rare in societies that produce little alienation, but common in the families of alienated youths. In boys, it has been found to prevent identification with the father. Lacking a role model which they can accept, these boys do not acquire a comfortable masculine sexual identity in adolescence. This not only contributes to alienation, but may produce anxiety, lack of self-esteem, and fear and resentment of father-figures in society. In its extreme form, such a background can lead to homosexuality.

These qualities were prominent among the male users I have met: few of them felt comfortably sure of their physical, sexual, or emotional competence. Most, though not consciously searching for "masculinity," felt that they had never had a chance to prove themselves, that they needed to pass the tests of the school of hard knocks, to grapple with tough, down-to-earth things. For many, like Lauren, insecurity was reinforced by the dominating closeness of their mothers. Feeling trapped by their mothers, angered at not being allowed to grow up completely, they wanted to escape into the outside world to do so.

Girls, too, revolted against their mothers' domination, as in Paula's case. Though not faced with the issue of identification with their fathers, they had lacked the love of a close male figure in childhood. As a result, some of the girls I met seemed to be searching for father-substitutes among males in the drug world. "Groupies" — girls who idolize and sleep with rock singers — may be an extreme example of this.

Middle- to upper-class life as a whole contributes equally to the sense of shelter. Both boys and girls that I have met, including those who did not share the family background just discussed, realized that technology and affluence had shielded them from most physical and emotional hardships. They perceived, quite correctly, that they were ignorant of the trials which the other 95% of the world's people face daily. Often they envied those who had led a tough life, who had experienced the "real thing." Guilty in their comfortable environment and doubtful of their ability to deal with the world on their own, these youths sought challenges to make their lives more demanding, ways to test their competence in the unsheltered world. Often this began with moderate drug use and continued to the extremes of running away, joining the street scene, and dealing drugs.

Drugs as a Test

For most, the process of self-testing begins long before the decision to drop out of school. For boys who are not too uncomfortable with their identities, it may never approach that point; they may be content to demonstrate their competence at driving, drinking, sex, or other conventional activities. Even smoking marijuana is approaching the conventional; in many high schools and colleges, the student who has not used it, statistically speaking, is deviant. The majority may treat him as a sheepish, inhibited, unsophisticated, or even slightly eccentric individual. In a word, marijuana is no longer cool; a youth who really wants to prove himself must go further.

LSD is ideal for this, for although it has become almost commonplace in some areas, it is still a formidable experience to have weathered a few bad trips, grappled with the fear of death, and coped with difficult real-life situations while tripping. Even those who treat LSD very lightly derive a sense of accomplishment from this, and many have told me that they valued their bad trips more than their good ones. A veteran of fifty trips named Peter described this:

> The pleasant things that happen to you on acid are very nice, but the times that really mattered to me were when I started getting into trouble. I remember the first time I got into a real horror show — I was all alone in my room, and I'd been tripping about two hours, when suddenly all the colors in the room started looking more and more sinister, and all these bugs started appearing in front of my eyes. The ashtray turned into a big cockroach and started crawling across the table to me, and spots on my pants turned into these really ugly little white bugs, and they started coming out of the wall, and out from under the rug, and crawling toward me from all over the room. I just sat there, frozen, for what seemed like hours, watching them. It was like in a dream. I was so scared that I couldn't even move my mouth to scream. Then, somewhere in the depths of my mind, something said, "It's you who has manufactured those bugs. They're just a projection onto the outside world of all the hostility you feel inside yourself." And when I had that realization, the bugs vanished in a tenth of a second. I learned more from that moment than I did from ten good trips.

The same reasoning will sometimes lead drug users to try a hallucinogen which they know is very likely to be unpleasant, such as belladonna. An even better example is a noxious mixture of unknown composition that circulated in 1968 named, not surprisingly, "LBJ." Everyone knew that it was a guaranteed bad trip (it was said that the dealer would refund your money if the experience was too pleasant), but many people tried it, just to have passed the test.

The reverence for bad trips, however, is much less common among younger users, who may become very blasé about LSD. A high-school boy caught the flavor of this in describing a typical scene in his home town:

> There are like six people sitting in a room tripping, and grooving on the pretty colors, and suddenly Jane starts getting into something heavy. She begins to realize that acid is a bigger thing than just seeing colors, and she begins to get deep into it and get frightened. Then somebody looks over and grins and says, "Whassa matta, Jane, you freak-ing out?" And either she snaps back into the seeing colors thing or she gets real frightened and never takes acid again.

Not only are the younger users less impressed by their bad trips, but they do not seem to get them as often. Perhaps this is because they treat hallucinogens more lightly, or it may be that they experience less of a shattering of personality than an older user with more years of organizing his ego and his defenses. At any rate, the big hallucinogens are not really an adequate test for many of the younger users, and for this reason — conscious or unconscious — some take heroin.

Heroin is not nearly as exciting as hallucinogens. It feels vaguely like being drunk on a stiff dose of very good hard liquor. Emotions are annihilated; someone could walk in and die on the floor and one would go on nodding and quietly contemplating the ceiling. Though the first dose one shoots is often quite frightening, heroin does not pack the horrors and thrills of a heavy LSD trip. But still it is cool; the needle has always separated the tough guys from the timid ones in the drug world. Many high school students, however much they may talk about the stupidity and the danger of "shooting skag," are a little bit impressed with it. If a boy is seeking to prove himself, the unspoken admiration of his peers can be practically addictive in itself.

The Death-Rebirth Trip

Along the scale of drug tests, from the first puff of marijuana to heavy use of heroin, LSD seems to hold a special place, particularly in the minds of older users. No single drug experience so sharply divides those who are initiated from those who are not. Among LSD users, this is revealed by their attitude toward novices. Long ago, my college friend, Cory, talking to a heavy user in Boston named Dick, mentioned that I would like to meet him. According to Cory's account, one of the first questions Dick asked was, "Has this cat ever done acid?" Cory said that he thought I had not. Dick's expression changed, and he said, "How does he expect to know where it's at? He can't understand anything about this scene until he's done acid a few times. I mean, it's so hard to talk to anyone who hasn't tripped." When I later met Dick, he was distinctly more distant from me than others have been.

A more immediate situation, but with similar implications, occurred when I came from uptown to the apartment on the Lower East side described at the beginning of this book. It was the first night I spent there. One boy, Bob, asked me if I would like to shoot up some LSD. "Hell, man, I'd love to," I replied, "but I've got four final exams back in college a week from today and I can't risk being spaced out when I take them." Bob was visibly disappointed. He pointed around the room: "I'm tripping, and he is, and he is, and she is, and he is, and she is, and he is. Are you *sure* you don't want to take any?" It was painfully obvious that I was the only outsider. When I still declined, I lost some of my rapport with all of them and never quite regained it with two or three.

To be sure, situations like this one occur in other drug subcultures, and I have experienced an even more serious loss of rapport by refusing alcohol at gatherings euphemistically called "happy hours". But I have never seen such a clear separation of outsiders, so definite a sense of division between the novices and the initiated, as among LSD users.

Alienated boys in this country could well use a *bona fide* initiation rite to give them a sense of competence and and masculinity, to put a premium on adulthood and commitment, to provide a sense of identity. Such trivial initiations as entering college, getting a driver's license, or joining a fraternity do not begin to fill this need; they have none of the power of a real initiation rite. But the LSD trip does. Though not as meaningful an initiation as in 1966, when it was more exotic than today, LSD still is a tremendous psychological experience. Like secret primitive initiation rites, it is something that cannot, almost must not, be described to the novice; it can only be experienced. In high doses, it may mimic another common feature of initiation rites, a symbolic death and rebirth. On LSD, the experience is far more than symbolic; the total dissolution of the ego is often felt as an actual bodily death and rebirth. I can remember one heavy user who remarked after a 1000 microgram trip, "I died three times last night". One of the most tantalizing things about high-dose LSD is the hope, conscious or unconscious, that when the rebirth comes, it will be into a beautiful, new and more meaningful world.

The parallel can be extended further. Whiting and others have argued that in societies in which a boy has been raised by women or otherwise acquired a feminine identity, a traumatic initiation rite serves to "brainwash" the old identity and substitute a masculine one. High-dose LSD is probably intense enough to accomplish a similar brainwashing. Indeed, many of the fathers of LSD use in this country, such as Leary and Alpert, claim that one can acquire a new personality pattern during the experience by imprinting, just as Konrad Lorenz's baby ducks could learn to identify any moving object as their mother.

Among younger male users, the desire for initiation through LSD is rarely expressed in words. They do not speak of imprinting or brainwashing their old identities, nor do they talk about masculinity, *per se.* But the unconscious need for initiation persists — they still draw a sharp line between themselves and those who have not used LSD, they still define it as a step away from shelter and out into the world, and occasionally someone derives from a death-rebirth trip a powerful sense of initiation.

The Street Scene

For some, even the most frightening and demanding of drug experiences are inadequate tests. They are the youths who run away, seeking in the "real world" a more genuine challenge for themselves. Cory, the boy quoted earlier, felt this acutely:

> You know I've been going with another guy to a spade bar in Central Square. And it's so different from all of the people here. Those people live and love their way through every minute of life, Skip. A guy is measured there by the quickness of his repartees and his fists, and how much alcohol he can hold, and whether or not he's ever shot up skag. I can't go on in this nice, quiet life in college until I've seen how I shape up in that world.

Soon after the time of this conversation, Cory left college. His story is a very, very common one: a boy who feels dominated by his mother, unable to accept or identify with his father, and uncomfortable with his sheltered surroundings, drops out of school to test himself in the real world. And the parents, tragically, never seem to realize how necessary this step appeared to him, and how much courage it took to make it.

For the runaway, the street scene is a demanding test of toughness. Besides the drug experiences themselves, he faces the challenge of surviving in a distant city, not knowing where the next meal (or, for that matter, the next bath) is coming from, sleeping in abandoned buildings, facing the threats of police on one side and "rip-off artists" on the other. As a boy from the Cambridge street scene recently said to me,

> You come from medical school where everything is easy for you. You get your meals served at the same time each day, and your room heated for you in the winter. And nobody ever hassles you, or mugs you in your apartment and rips off everything you own. But out here in the cold, it's *life,* man. You learn about what it's really like to be on your own, to really have to find out about yourself. The street scene is where it's at man — you've got to come out here and live it for a while.

Even back in 1968, when the street scene was much less malignant than today, my good friend Bill described it similarly:

> But you don't understand, Skip. The drugs and the sex and lying in the sun on the grass are not what's important. It's having to eat the roast beef you found in the garbage can, and getting sick off it, and not having a place to crash at night. That's what these people are really here to learn.

Having put themselves to the test, most of the street people surprise themselves with their resourcefulness; they find that they can make it in the school of hard knocks. In the summer of 1968, for instance, Ron, one of the boys who frequently crashed in my apartment, made friends with the night baker at the doughnut shop down the street. Often we would wake up and find Ron already at the breakfast table, whittling away at a pile of sixty or seventy day-old doughnuts which he had obtained at three o'clock that morning. We usually finished about twenty ourselves and took the rest to the Common, where they disappeared, in about five minutes, into the mouths of other hungry hippies.

The ultimate test of a male's toughness and competence is to become what is known to many youths as a "greaser." Greasers are not only users and dealers of hard-core drugs such as barbiturates, heroin, and cocaine, but they live an entire life style of asserting masculinity. A friend of mine from Philadelphia described them as follows:

> Most of them had bikes, and they had a lot more sex than the other guys. Or at least they talked like they did. These guys always carried knives around — they'd just as soon kill you as speak to you, you know. And they were into a lot of alcohol, a lot of skag, anything they could get their hands on.

I have met quite a few of these types, many of them of working-class background, but some from very affluent homes. In fact, of the three I knew best, two had fathers who ranked high in the armed services. One named Rick, whom I saw frequently until he stole $50 from me, had been jailed about six times, usually for smashing somebody in a barroom brawl. He frequently came to Boston and New York, where he obtained hallucinogens and amphetamines to sell in his native Chicago. Rick was present one night when a boy from Boston introduced his girlfriend to marijuana.

> "You realize that the first puff has committed you irrevocably on the road to heroin addiction?" someone kidded her.
> "And the fact is, it does!" Rick laughed.

He rolled up his sleeve to show two veins blistered with needle tracks. The poor girl was rather disconcerted.

Rick seemed to like me, although he never got to know me very well. I can remember that he once said to me:

> Skip, if anybody up in Boston gives you trouble, I can always arrange to get them taken care of for you. I got lots of friends in Chicago who would just love to break somebody's arms. All you have to do is pay their plane fare to Boston, and give them fifty dollars apiece.

Although I never availed myself of his offer, I am quite sure that it was genuine.

The most extraordinary thing about Rick's life was that his parents were pathetically ignorant of what was going on. They were not even aware of the name by which he was known in the drug world; someone used it once in calling him at home and was told by his mother that it must be a wrong number. His parents were astonished when they accidently found eight hundred insulin syringes in the trunk of the little car that they had given to their supposedly well-behaved teenager. Even then, they apparently refused to believe that he was really involved in such activities.

Another greaser I knew was a seventeen-year-old named Melvin who came from an affluent New York suburb. Melvin's life style reflected, more clearly than Rick's, his reaction-formation against a sheltered childhood. Having long ago run away from his wealthy home, he spent his time riding his motorcycle, sleeping with girls, getting drunk, and shooting heroin. When not involved in these activities, he went out of his way to recount them to others. Perhaps the most interesting story he told me was about setting off a quarter of a stick of dynamite in the high school gym in his town shortly before the June prom. It blew a crater in the floor and smashed every one of the two-hundred-odd window panes in the room. I originally assumed, of course, that this story was a put-on, but I later heard it independently from another boy, named Jim, who had attended the same high school. Jim did not know Melvin, but he said that the dynamite incident was characteristic of the alcohol-amphetamine-heroin group there, which went to great lengths to demonstrate its toughness.

This is the extreme of the wide range of responses to the sheltered life: from "blowing dope" after school, through hallucinogens, to heroin, and from running away from home and school to big dealing and a violent, aggressive life-style. For some, the tests of drug use, or the initiations of multiple death-rebirth trips, provide a satisfying sense of accomplishment, of having grown up. But a few drug tests cannot erase the insecurities acquired in years of childhood; most users continue to seek, in further drug use and in their lives as a whole, new challenges, new experiences to test their competence.

V. ANGER AND WITHDRAWAL

Baiting the Establishment

As already discussed, most of the users I have met described their fathers as distant and unemotional. In addition, even those users who did not experience this at home discovered it among authority figures in American society. Through personal experience or the media they encountered teachers, law officials and politicians who condemned the irrational or emotional components in campus violence, antiwar demonstrations and other dissent without attempting to understand them. And even before they had tried drugs themselves, many of these youths were shocked at the older generation's failure to understand drug use, not only factually, but emotionally. They reacted with anger, occassionally directed at their fathers specifically, but more often at authority as a whole.

Theories of the origins of the emotional generation gap can be found in the literature on alienation; as to the anger it provokes, no description is needed. Radicalism is the most common way of dealing with this anger, but drug use can also serve this purpose, as suggested by the following accounts from four different users:

> Half of the fun of grass and acid are that they're illegal. If they suddenly became legal, the bottom would drop right out of the whole scene. You know in some ways I hope they never do become legal.

> Hey guys, guess what? I just committed my first capital offense! I just sold skag to a guy under 18!

> Boy it really pisses me off now when I see those anti-drug ads that the government puts on TV. You see some chick smoke dope, and then she writhes around on the floor and hallucinates and so on. And then they show you the same thing happen to someone on acid. So you go out and try some dope, and it turns out to be much milder than alcohol. And you do acid, and that turns out to be the most beautiful thing you've ever seen. And so you begin to realize how much bullshit they've been feeding you, so you go on and do speed and coke and skag, and they turn out to be nice, too. Every time I see one of those ads on TV now, it really makes me mad. I'd like to go out and turn on some more kids, just to show them how they're being put on.

> You know what finally got me to take acid? I saw one of those mail trucks go by with a thing on the side saying, "Will you turn on to drugs or will drugs turn on you?" I decided that if they had to go that far to convince you not to take acid, it must be a pretty good thing, so I tried it.

At times it seems that the angrier the campaign to prevent drug use, the more users it starts. Perhaps this is because potential users perceive, consciously or unconsciously, envy behind the inflated hostility of their worst opponents. A girl from California described this explicitly:

> Everybody knows that they wouldn't put you in jail for twenty years unless they were afraid you were having too much fun. And what's really pathetic is when they send some "expert" to tell you that dope dilates your pupils, which it doesn't, or that it causes risk of insanity. Their whole response to it is so obviously irrational that it really exposes them.

A former college student at Berkeley also sensed envy in the older generation:

> The old-time hippies really hit that soft spot in the Establishment. The Establishment knows how to repond to violence — they're much better at violence than we are. But what really shakes them up, the thing that they really don't know how to deal with, is the idea that you're getting more sex than they are, and having more fun than they are, and being more alive than they are. Suddenly the American middle class looks around and realizes that all of their money, and all their possessions are worthless. And of course they don't admit this to themselves. Instead, they decide that since you've stayed in the park past curfew, that they have an excuse to send the pigs after you. And you throw flowers at the pigs, and then they're *really* confused. They've never had this happen to them before. And you lie down on the grass and force them to drag you away. Man, if we had had a Gandhi to lead us in those days, we could have turned the United States upside down faster than all revolutionaries and all the demonstrations in the world.

By 1968, most of the old-time hippies were gone. Lacking a Gandhi, they had disappeared into apartments in the city and communes in the country. One of the few who remained was a boy from Michigan named Kim, one of the warmest, most loving human beings I have met. Kim weighed about one-hundred-ten pounds, soaking wet, but he was arrested after the curfew hour for assaulting a two-hundred-pound police officer. Once in the paddy wagon, the "assault" turned into a sexual assault on Kim, a fact that was independently confirmed to me by two other people who rode in the van and looked on, too scared to intervene. I doubt that that policeman (who, they discovered, was married and the father of two) was the only member of the force to be dissatisfied with his sex life at home.

Kim's act of staying in the park after curfew, like drug use, was a passive expression of anger: a way of eliciting and exposing anger and envy in the Establishment without being violent in itself. When this technique really works, it can be very satisfying, an effective way to act out anger. One evening, for instance, Ron (the boy who got the day-old doughnuts), with three others, all wearing the clothes that they had been wearing for the last month, walked up to the desk clerk at the Ritz Carlton hotel.

> "We're looking for a place to crash for the night," said Ron.

> "Our cheapest room is twenty dollars," snarled the clerk.

> "But nobody is going to use it tonight if we don't, are they?" said Ron. "So we'll sleep on the floor instead of the bed, and then you won't have to clean up anything after we leave!"

> "I'm afraid that's impossible."

> "What do you mean, it's impossible? It's perfectly possible. You want me to demonstrate?"

> "I'm sorry but — "

> "Where's the manager? I want to talk to the manager!"

> "All right, you *will* talk to the manager!" said the clerk, beginning to quiver visibly.

But the manager fared little better than the clerk, and predictably, faced with a situation that violated his social expectations, he threatened to call the police.

Ron and his friends threatened that *they* were going to go get the police themselves and walked out, barely able to conceal their laughter. It was so much fun that they wandered over to the Statler Hilton and did it again, raising an ever greater uproar until they were evicted by an army of bellhops. And by the time they reached the Sheraton Plaza later in the evening, it was down to a science — they almost got themselves a room!

Those were the good old days, when shaking up the Establishment was still, on occasion, humorous. But there is another passive expression of anger which is not humorous. This is when the anger is turned inward and drug use becomes a form of deliberate self-destructiveness. Self-destructiveness may serve various psychological functions: atoning for guilt, directing at one's own body the anger felt toward the outside world, or proving, through one's own demise, the evils of one's society and upbringing. The last case is illustrated in an account from a boy who injects 900 mg. of amphetamine per day:

> Listen, man, I know that speed kills, I know that it only takes three years before your brain is rotted into a bloody pulp. Hell, I can already feel my memory beginning to go. But that's how it is. There isn't anything else that's worth doing in this fucking world, nothing else that I can get into, anyhow. I'll have a few good times in those three years. That's all I can expect. I don't want any damned people coming around trying to rehabilitate me. It's my choice and that's how I'm going to live. And if my parents find me, they can just go screw. They all ought to realize just how sick they've made this world.

Drug users, unlike radicals, tend to express anger in passive ways such as these: using drugs to express opposition to anti-drug campaigns, attempting to expose violence and envy in the Establishment, and sometimes, punishing their parents, their society, and themselves by self-destructiveness. Many, like Lauren, play along with society in the "official ways" — graduate from high school with a minimum of work, get a psychiatric deferment rather than resist the draft, let mother think that it is by accident that they are spilling gravy at dinner — and express the anger covertly by using bigger drugs and quietly dropping out.

Dropping Out

Dropping out is a complex act. Superficially, especially for boys, it is a rejection of the "masculine" or "success-oriented" values in our culture that are usually represented by the father: short hair, drab clothes, especially suits and ties, athletics, competitiveness, aggression, and sometimes heterosexuality. But there is something more to it than that, in both girls and boys — a rejection of our whole cultural emphasis on hard-boiled rationality and mental control, our denunciation of mysticism and deification of technology. Many drug users view rationality and "ego control" as a curse; they want to "blow their minds," to retreat into some non-rational state, be it produced by LSD, heroin, cough syrup, or model airplane glue. Much of this is due to being on the rebound from a hyperrational and mechanically oriented society, but the psychoanalyst would argue that it also represents a wish to abandon the "reality principle" in favor of an earlier state of closeness with the mother. This desire reaches the ultimate expression in the "return to the womb" of the fusion experience: it was perhaps more instinctive than conscious that Henry clutched his arms around his knees as he hung underwater in the pool.

One of the consequences of the retreat from rationality is an interest in mysticism and the occult: astrology, astral projection, tarot cards, Eastern philosophies, the *I Ching,* witchcraft, and sorcery. Even those techniques which have some scientific basis, such as macrobiotics, yoga, and meditation, draw much appeal from the fact that they promise relief from the no-nonsense technicality of our culture, and offer a hope of a mystic, egoless state beyond.

LSD, once again, answers these feelings because, even in moderate doses, the effects are — to coin a word — "pedomimetic," meaning that they simulate the feelings of early childhood. Pleasure-principle thinking (referred to as primary process) substantially replaces the usually dominant reality-principle thinking (called secondary process since it is learned). The ego, in both the popular and the psychoanalytic senses, is progressively impaired with larger doses until, at about 500 clinical micrograms, there is little reality left. The effect on cognition is much more global than that of marijuana or alcohol; it is as if the whole world had suddenly become weird; the novice can easily forget that it is all caused by a tiny crystal and that he will be "real" again in a few hours. And yet, although the experience is extraordinarily novel and alien to nonpsychotic individuals, many of them have a sense of "deja vu," as if somewhere they have seen it all before. This too may be evidence for the pedomimetic model, as are the descriptions of users such as these three:

For four hours I felt mentally like a four-year-old.

Tripping in Boston feels like when you are very, very

young, and your mother takes you to the city. You ride on the subway and get scared, and you look up at the buildings and everything is huge and beautiful. There is so much going on that you can't even begin to understand it.

My first bad trip felt just like when I was a little kid trying to fall asleep in a dark room. There was a crocodile under the bed, and if you didn't jump into bed in a certain way, he would bite you, and there were ghosts behind the curtains and burglars about to come in the window. Just like when I was a child, part of me knew it wasn't real, but the other half of me was scared as hell!

Another account is from a psychiatrist, experienced with drug-using patients, one of many who believe that people have taken LSD to withdraw into an early childhood state:

I had a boy, a couple of years ago, who told me that while on LSD, he had seen a huge spider walk up to him, and that he had turned himself into a gorilla and defeated the spider. This is a clear-cut example of almost pure primary process thought. The spider, of course, represents his mother. . . .

The egoless state of LSD thought is certainly not always pleasurable, but for many users, there is something about it that is preferable to ego domination; they want to escape from the curse of the rational, to leave their cut-and-dried, scientific, everything-is-explained world and live for awhile in a magical one. The wish is old as mankind, and it has never in the past been so effortlessly satisfied as it is now with hallucinogens. It is reminiscent of a button I once saw on the lapel of a psychology student, which read, "Take the lid off your id!"

The LSD trip may well be the best facsimile of early childhood and even intrauterine experiences, but the many who seek sheer remoteness from reality can go even further on substances available at the corner drug store: "Romilar" cough syrup, powdered belladonna leaf ("Asthmador"), intravenous "Ban" deodorant, and that old standby, airplane glue, which is occasionally used even by ten-year-olds.

The following account, from a prep-school boy named Bert, indicates how effectively one can incapacitate the ego with glue:

> "Well, we went downtown and bought a model kit and a thing of glue. The model kit was just an excuse so that the guy in the store wouldn't ask questions. Then you put the glue in a paper bag and cover your face with it, and start breathing. After a minute or two you start feeling a little drunk, and then you suddenly realize that with every breath you are getting further and further from reality. And after a few more breaths, there is absolutely *nothing* — no past, present, future, time, meaning, existence — just *nothing*. What happened to me was that I ran screaming down the corridor and down the stairs and I started pounding on my faculty adviser's door. Then I collapsed on the floor. He came out, looked around, didn't look down, and miraculously closed the door without seeing me. I guess he must have thought it was a bunch of guys pounding on his door and then running away. At any rate, I was beginning to come to my senses by that point, and I realized how close I'd come to getting kicked out of the school."

> "Why did you do glue in the first place?"

> "Just to blow my mind, I guess."

No one simple explanation exists as to why Bert wanted to blow his mind that afternoon. Some students at his school, sick of its scholarly atmosphere and excessive restrictions, might have expressed their frustrations with anger. But for Bert and many of his classmates it was possible only to withdraw: the few moments of insanity were a welcome release from an environment of intellectuality and competition.

VI. LONELINESS AND COMMUNITY

Looking for "The Commune"

Previous chapters have described the responses of individual youths to American society and to their family backgrounds. But drug use is not an individual phenomenon. It occurs in groups, and much of its appeal stems from its interpersonal elements. These are most important in perpetuating drug use once it has started. But loneliness is also an initial reason for using drugs and for leaving home.

Many adults, curiously, assume that if a youth is lonely, it is entirely his fault. A few months ago, for instance, a lady at a cocktail party said to me:

> It's a shame, you know. All these kids have their whole class at school to associate with, and they live in a nice neighborhood with lots of other kids like themselves. If they're lonely, it's their fault, there's got to be something wrong with them.

This lady's assumptions reflect suburbia's preoccupation with privacy. She accepted as given that everyone would want his own house, his own car, his own television set. If a boy had the choice, why should he want to live in a cramped little apartment with five other people? Surely there must be something wrong with him.

Values are quite different in an urban, working-class neighborhood which enjoys an ethnic identity. Recently a family I know, the Ryans, moved out of their neighborhood in Roxbury to live in the suburbs. A month after the move, I asked Mrs. Ryan how she liked her new town. She said:

> Oh, Skip, it's so quiet! I can't stand it! There's nobody around to talk to, and nobody running around on the street. I really miss hearing all the children playing outside. On our street down there, there's only one other family that has children the same age as my kids. I suppose it's good for the kids' education, and so on, that we moved out there, but I almost want to move back. It's so lonely!

Mrs. Ryan could easily sympathize with a suburban youth who wanted to live in a crowded apartment in the city. But parents who have spent much of their lives in the pursuit of privacy rarely understand why their children should feel that there is something missing, that a community instinct has never quite been satisfied. In some youths, the feeling is so acute that it becomes the major reason for leaving home: they come to the city, looking for "the commune," for a closeness with people that they have not experienced before. But unfortunately, the transition is difficult: if they join a commune, they are surprised to discover that they have learned too well some of their parents' ideas of property and privacy.

Loneliness and the need for community are often hard to express, perhaps because they are largely on an instinctive level; for many, such as the girl in the Beatles' song, it is a sensation of "something inside that was always denied." But I can remember two friends who did try to define it. The first was a college student:

> One of the most beautiful memories in all my life was the time that I spent with these other guys in Texas,

looking for peyote cactuses. We drove around in an old, broken-down VW bus, for about four thousand miles, sleeping out in the desert, or sometimes driving all night, with two guys up front and two asleep in the back. There was something indescribably wonderful about that time, something that I have felt only a few times in my life, the feeling of being with a gang of guys, a feeling of real unity, of a male bond. It wasn't without hardships, of course, like the time Mayer fell asleep on a curve and drove us about two hundred yards into the desert in the dead of night. But even the bad things were fun.

And of course, the best thing of all was when we finally discovered the peyote patch up in Big Bend, and we each ate four fresh buttons. I have tripped on a lot of things a lot of times, but that trip was unquestionably the most beautiful that I have ever had. In the afternoon, we went to the Rio Grande and stripped down and went swimming for about two hours, hallucinating all the time, and then lay in the hot sun on the riverbank and got our asses so sunburned that we could hardly sit down. And in the evening we climbed a hill on the Mexican side and watched the sun set. We could all feel the same uncanny feeling of unity with one another — each of us could just sense it in the others. We were so euphoric that we stayed up talking and telling stories until six o'clock the next morning, and it wasn't until after the sun came up that we finally fell asleep.

You know, I never had times of closeness like that when I was younger; even though I had lots of friends, I was still subtly isolated from other people. Taking drugs, and experiences like that one in Texas, are helping me to break out of the loneliness and really love people.

The second was a girl named Joan, who joined a commune after she graduated from high school:

When we first started the commune two years ago, it was really tough. We would spend hours each week talking about what food we were going to buy for the next week, and who was going to pay what, and who would have to wash the dishes and clean up the living room. And we all got angry at each other, and a couple of people left, but the rest of us stuck it out, because we knew that we were on the right track, that what we had going was more important than all the little hassles that were hanging us up. And we were right, because now it's almost two years later, and we really have a good thing going. It's not perfect — we all get mad at each other once in a while, but it's a beautiful thing to come home to after being away for a week, and see nine other people who all really know you and love you. You know, I don't think I would ever care to return to the other way and live in a little house with my husband and a couple of kids. It would just be unnatural, somehow. Maybe time will prove me wrong, but I doubt it.

This story, alas, is an unusual one, for most communes do not succeed as well. The prompt gratification and "do your own thing" ethos of the drug world conflicts with communal needs, not only in doing the dishes, but in being responsible and caring towards other people. Few groups that I have seen achieved the instinctive warmth and mutual understanding of Joan's, or had the perseverance to make it through the difficulties of the first year. But now that the commune is working, I think that most of its members would agree with Joan — they would not want to live their lives or raise their children in any other way. They are no longer lonely.

Sex

Not all drug users deal so directly with their loneliness, because not all loneliness is generated externally. Some of it is a consequence of the typical family background already described. The effects of this background, and the reasons that it produces loneliness, are illustrated in users' sexual behavior.

One afternoon on the Boston Common, in the summer of 1968, two businessmen in suits threaded their way through the crowds of hippies sitting on the path. One of them accosted a policeman on the corner and said:

"Can't you do anything about all these ragamuffins blocking the paths? Lousy, no good, dirty kids, too lazy to get a job. The city is going to end up paying for all of them!"

"Can't do anything unless you want to write a formal complaint, sir," replied the policeman.

Ignoring him, the businessman continued to mutter.

"They think they can just sit around and play all day, and then at night — Oh, I just don't know!"

Without allowing the policeman to reply, he stormed away, throwing a final, angry glance at the crowd. It was curious that he had hesitated at the words "at night." If they played all day, what did they do all night, while he watched television and did his homework from the office? What sexual fantasies lurked behind that extraordinarily angry glance?

Had he known the truth, he might not have been quite so furious about the "ragamuffins" on the path, for they were not getting as much sex as he supposed. For example, two afternoons later, a group of us were walking through the South End when we noticed a movie marquis which proclaimed, "Hippie Love-In."

"Hey, Bill," said one, "you ever been to a love-in?"

"No. Have you?"

"No. I haven't. Maybe we'd all better buy tickets and find out what it's like!"

This is a typical story; hippie love-ins, alas, are much more common in the movies, or, for that matter, in the fantasies of the hippies themselves, than in real life. The great majority of the users I knew followed a pattern of "serial monogamy" no different from countless youths who do not take drugs: they stayed with one member of the opposite sex for a period of months or even years, then began a new relationship or sometimes got married. Though many of them had slept with a partner for just one or two nights, a comparable number had had intercourse with only one or two partners in their lives. Some high school users had had no sexual experience at all. A few users, particularly the greasers, described very wide heterosexual experiences, but they accounted for less than a tenth of the total group that I have known.

Many of my friends had little interest in promiscuity; they were more interested in establishing deep, loving relationships than in scoring a high number of sexual contacts. But a larger number were not satisfied with their heterosexual activity; they felt that they did not meet as many partners as they wished. For boys in particular, the limiting factor was anxiety or guilt stemming from their close relationships with their mothers. And even those boys not inhibited by such feelings had to cope with the high ratio of boys to girls in the drug world. This was fine for the girls, who often had a great deal of heterosexual experience. But the boys, unable to find an uninvolved girl in their own subculture, were forced to meet more conventional girls back at school or college, which was often difficult, since these girls had different interests and different circles of friends. Sex, which has been the solution to both boredom and loneliness in primitive societies since time immemorial, did not replace drugs in this function in the street scene.

Homosexuality, on the other hand, was much more prevalent among drug users than is believed by the general public or even by many of the users themselves. In my statistical study of college drug users already cited, one in seven of the male heavy users reported a homosexual experience to orgasm *since coming to college,* a figure more than six times as great as for the non-users. For those who have dropped out of high school or college, the figure is certainly higher; among the boys on Boston Common in 1968, it was probably over 20%. Homosexuality was also quite common among the girls, but the total group of girls that I knew was too small to allow a good estimate of its prevalence. Very few of the boys or the girls were *exclusively* homosexual, however; some had experimented with it only briefly, and most of the rest had acquired a good deal of experience with both sexes.

The incidence of homosexuality is hardly surprising, for it satisfies many of the same feelings discussed as origins of drug use. For boys, as already mentioned, it may be a reaction to the extreme case of the family constellation of a distant father and a dominant, intimate mother. For both sexes, it is a reaction to anger: like drug use, it has the thrill of the forbidden. And it serves, as it always has through the ages, as a way of dealing with loneliness; for example, as a compensation for not having had "buddies" when one was younger. Finally, it is a response to the entire drug subculture's approval of acting out. Homosexual *desire* may not be tremendously greater among drug users, but they have had more opportunity and more encouragement actually to do something about it.

Drugs as an Answer to Loneliness

The companionship of other users, then, provides an initial answer to loneliness: the life of a commune instead of the privacy of a suburban community, and the hope of a greater amount of heterosexual and homosexual satisfaction. In short, the *first* effect of loneliness is to bring a youth into association with users. Once he has joined the group, the drugs themselves provide further ways of relating to others and dealing with sexual desires.

To begin with, drug use is a good way to meet people. To take a drug with someone is often the first step in getting to know him or her. Perhaps this is why Bob, on the Lower East Side, was so disturbed when I did not take LSD with him and the others; I had rejected one of his best expressions of friendship. For some, this is an absolute prerequisite for friendship; if a person refuses to take drugs with them, they will not attempt to relate in another way. One may say that this is neurotic, but he must remember the millions of friendships in this country that began with the ritualized interchange of nicotine. So, too, for alcohol: suppose one were to offer a drink to a stranger in a bar, only to have him decline and order a tall glass of ice water instead. One would probably draw the same conclusion that a marijuana user would in an analogous situation – the man must be from the FBI.

Drugs are also a way of breaking down inhibitions, especially with the opposite sex. Alcohol, again, is the time-honored agent for this purpose; most adults in our society are familiar with its virtues. But equally popular among the young are amphetamines, (Benzedrine, Dexedrine, Methedrine, "speed"), which, like alcohol, produce a hangover and are physically harmful in large doses. But they are not nearly as addictive, interfere much less with coordination or driving, and seem to sharpen the mind rather than dull it. They are ideal for meeting other people, because they make one aggressive, confident, euphoric, and above all, talkative:

> I just took four of those orange tabs of dex, and I feel beautiful! If only I could feel this way all the time — this is the way all human beings ought to feel all the time — this is what it feels like to be a real human being — a *real human being!* Are you listening to me? You were beginning to look a little bored. . . . This is how everybody ought to feel — I mean, I can just walk up to anybody I want to — anybody — some chick I've never seen before, and just start rapping — I've got that extra boost of self-confidence. I feel like I'd just like to go around to people and tell them how much I love them — how much I enjoy talking to them — it's just beautiful! I really want to talk to people! I really do!

I have known many youths like this who used amphetamines specifically to meet other people, or to "get into the heads" of people they already knew.

For getting deeper into somebody's head, the ultimate drug, once again, is LSD. This is not always the case; some people, especially inexperienced users, will spend all of their time quietly free-associating and watching the colors, communicating only with an occasional "Oh, wow!" But for those who are more serious about their hallucinogens, particularly when tripping with only one or two friends, communication can be a moving and lasting experience. Long ago, when LSD users told me of this, I was suspicious of it. But when my close friends first took the drug, I sometimes had the impression that I was really seeing them for the first time, talking to them on a more intimate level than ever before. In retrospect, there is nothing particularly remarkable about this; it is simply due to the impossibility of maintaining one's ordinary defenses when the ego has been impaired. Not surprisingly, those who have experienced this communication return to LSD again and again and often recommend it to their friends as a way to cure interpersonal "hassles."

The users of amphetamines and LSD, then, do not differ much from users of nicotine and alcohol. Both are following the ancient and universal practice of making friends through the interchange and mutual use of drugs. But there is a special case of loneliness in which drug users follow a newer, perhaps more peculiarly American tradition: that of substituting something material for sexual satisfaction. In the older generation, when perseverance, influence, and affluence fail to deal with frustration, the drug is alcohol. In the younger generation the choice of chemicals is wider. Marijuana and the hallucinogens are appropriate; sexuality is certainly implicit in the symbolic act of returning to childhood closeness with the mother, already discussed. But many users have acknowledged the wisdom of their elders and returned to alcohol or to a drug with somewhat similar effects, heroin, which if one buys in quantity from a decent source, is cheaper than good whiskey. Sexual frustration is infrequently a specific reason for taking hallucinogens, but it is not uncommon among those who embark on heavy opiate or barbiturate use. If sexual frustration is understood to include all of the boredom which may be related to it, then it becomes an undeniable basis for all drug use.

Finally, two or more people may use drugs together as a substitute for sexual interaction when it is precluded by anxiety or taboos. I can remember, for example, one boy who said to me, "Taking LSD with another guy is the closest you can get to overt homosexuality." He was aware of the feeling of sexual satisfaction in giving a drug to another person and seeing it give him pleasure. It is not an accident that to "turn on" a girl may refer to either giving her a drug or to sexually arousing her. This is one of the origins of drug users' almost universal urge to initiate new users.

The above are the more direct ways in which personal relationships, or the lack of them, may lead to drug use. General loneliness, or a search for sexual gratification, draws the potential user into the drug world. Once there, he may use drugs to initiate or deepen relationships, to deal with frustrations, or as a substitute for sexual interaction. But this chapter has only scratched the surface of the social aspects of drug use, for they become even more important after a youth has made the initial step of joining the subculture. We will return to this theme in chapter eight.

VII. THE SEARCH FOR ENLIGHTENMENT

Psychological Sophistication

The reader may already have noticed that the more eloquent drug users, particularly the older ones, use a striking amount of psychological and sociological terminology in their conversations. This is true even of many who have never had a formal course in these fields, such as Lauren, who could use words such as "obsessive-compulsive" and "projection" in his conversations. Psychological and sociological ideas also appear in Peter's comments about his bad trip (Chapter IV), in the descriptions of the envy of the older generation (Chapter V), and in other criticisms of the Establishment. Another example, in a letter from a boy in Michigan, might have been put in the fifth chapter under the "curse of the rational":

> Your anxiety ... is more a symptom of the rational
> ego control that tends to be ever-pervasive.

Another account, from a fifteen-year-old runaway in New York, might well go under "The Sheltered Life":

> I was trying to escape from the castrating effect of
> my home town. . . . The purpose of the school system
> was to make you into a compulsive worker, and your
> parents would reinforce this, to try to make you feel
> guilty when you didn't work. . . . I had to get out.

Of course, most fifteen-year-olds do not use so much
psychological jargon in ten minutes of talking, but practically every one
will use a little if asked why he dropped out. The jargon of the
subculture itself contains a number of "psychological" terms: hung up,
freaked out, ego trip, ego riff, game playing, mind games, and so forth.

Psychological ideas are also prominent in rock songs, such as
those by the Beatles or the Mothers of Invention, already cited, or in
"The End" by the Doors:

> Father
> Yes, son?
> I want to kill you!
> Mother! I want to —

The same can be found in many "underground" newspapers, such
as this old issue of *Open City* (1967, II: 20) in Los Angeles:

> He [the marijuana user] is generally a somewhat
> more perceptive person who knows that most people
> are engaged in shallow social games which barely
> cover the lonely desperation created by an unloving
> and economically exploitative society.

What are the origins of this interest in psychology and sociology?
First, it is due to the expansion of the science of psychology during the
last fifty years; it is no longer the esoteric field that it was in the past.
Today, most educated youths "believe in" Freud to at least some
extent, whereas in the 20's or even in the 40's, the Doors' song would
have sounded not only strange, but incomprehensible.

Secondly, the media have expanded, bringing psychological and
sociological ideas to people of all ages through movies, television
documentaries and social commentaries, and popular magazines
devoted to psychology. The effect of this is greatest among the young.

High school and college students talk about their "identity crises" and their sexuality to a degree which amazes their parents. And even younger children, though they do not learn anything of sociological theory, still have more of an overview of society than their parents had. In fact, David Riesman noticed the importance of this more than twenty years ago, even before the advent of television (Riesman 1950):

> From the mass media — radio, movies, comics — as well as their peers, [modern] children can easily learn what the norm of parental behavior is, and hold it over their parents' heads. (p. 50)

Finally, psychological sophistication is maximized in alienated youths, in many simply because they are well educated and have shown more interest in social sciences than in the so-called "hard" sciences. Also, as Keniston has pointed out, sophistication results from their own self-dissecting quality, an almost compulsive need to examine themselves and their relationships with others.

One of my ancestors used to say that "a little learning is a dang'rous thing." Such is often the case with psychological sophistication. It makes some youths unduly critical of themselves and their motives; they act as though it were inexcusable to have defenses, show aggression, or "play games." In others, conversely, it may provide rationalizations for personal qualities which really are problems, that do interfere with happiness. Finally, it provides intellectual reasons for rejecting the Establishment — usually perfectly *valid* reasons, perceptions of genuine evils, but nevertheless what the psychologist would call defenses of intellectualization, inasmuch as they conceal the crucial emotional basis for decisions. Psychological sophistication is not always harmful; it may produce valuable effects such as tolerance for others. Its mixed effect can be seen in the following account from a lesbian girl in Boston:

> "The reasons I'm so hung up are that my parents were very uptight, desperate people. They tried to live out all their unexpressed desires through me. The really frustrated one was my mother — she was completely incapable of living independently. She'd always need help at the smallest task — unscrewing a

jar or opening a window that had stuck a little bit. I'm sure that she had sexual desires for other women, but of course she was never able to express them."

"How do you feel about being homosexual?"

"Well, at first it made me uptight, but about three years ago, I suddenly realized that it was ridiculous to act as if it was wrong. In fact, it's much healthier for me to do it than to keep all those homosexual feelings bottled up inside me. *That* would be neurotic. In many societies, you know, women have sex with each other all the time, but in America, women are taught to suppress all their lesbian impulses."

"Do your parents know anything about it?"

"Yes, I eventually told my mother about it. And if it bothers her, that's tough shit. She ought to realize that I'm only reflecting her own hangups."

The intellectualizations in this case are more obvious than in most. Though they are defenses, they have a basis in truth: her "little learning" has freed her from a good deal of guilt and anxiety, but it has left her too complacent to examine her feelings in detail.

One Tablet Each Morning

Among drug users, the result of psychological sophistication is a sense of the futility of changing society. Even the youngest high school students are vaguely aware that social problems go deep into history and into the unconscious, that they are rarely cured by legislation, rational discussion, or the penitentiary. The result of this reasoning is an attempt, deliberate or unconscious, to *transform the self:* since it is hopeless to revolutionize society, the best one can do is drop out quickly and then purge the residue of evils that are left from one's upbringing in it. One statement of this, for example, is in "Revolution" by the Beatles:

> Well, you say you want to change institutions
> Well, you better change your minds instead.

It is at this point in the reasoning that many turn to LSD.

Since it reduces the ego to a childhood state, LSD actually works to some extent; it can wash away, at least temporarily, some of the learned behavior that the users want to eliminate. Most regular hallucinogen users feel that they have improved their personalities — that they are more loving, less defensive, less aggressive. Some of the more intellectual ones even take hallucinogens with the specific intent of curing their "hangups." For example, on one occasion in college, I saw a little bottle filled with tablets of LSD, on which someone had typed a neat label saying "LSD-25, 250 micrograms. One tablet each morning for neurosis." I have met many users, particularly older ones, who have great faith in the curative powers of LSD. They recommend it for frigidity, homosexuality, alcoholism, phobias, and many other ills. Interestingly, it has been used for all of these particular problems by professional psychiatrists, but with little more success than laymen: an occasional dramatic cure, and many failures.

Most users, of course, do not think of LSD as a specific psychotherapy for anything, but even those who take it "just for fun" show a little of the psychological orientation: they use it as a way of relating more deeply to other people, a way of escaping from the "bad" aspects of the ego, a way of erasing some of the "programming" that they feel they have received from society, and most of all, out of simple curiosity — to get a peek at their unconscious minds. Some who claim no personal therapeutic benefits have hopes that LSD will act as a sort of mass therapy for society, that the more people who take it, the faster things will change in favor of love and peace. For instance, a big dealer in Boston once said to me:

> We're going to try to make half a gram available for the march on Washington next week. Some day, down there, somebody's going to slip a few hundred mikes into the President's coffee, and then the world will really start to change! God put acid on earth right at this time because He saw that now it was most needed. This is where it had to appear in the order of things. And now that it's here, it's just going to grow until so many people have gotten turned on that all the hypocrisy and corruption in America will

just fall to pieces. And then nobody will go around
on an ego trip, killing off everybody who stands in his
way, hung up on possessions and power.

Will LSD make any changes in our society? Is it dangerous to get
a glimpse of one's unconscious? Has LSD injured more minds than it
has benefited? No one is beyond the "little learning" stage on these
questions. Some have argued that LSD might be a valuable tool in
psychology, but neither young nor old guarantees to reap the benefits
without incurring the disasters. The spread of psychological and
sociological knowledge among youth is analogous to that of nuclear
physics among nations: like the atom, LSD confers a mixed blessing on
those, driven by the hopes of greater understanding or by sheer
curiosity, who are bold enough to tamper with it.

Going East

Among the older or more intellectual users of hallucinogens, the search
for philosophical enlightenment ranks even higher than the search for
psychological insight; it is certainly better known to the general public.
Hallucinogens have been used as a source of religious experiences for
thousands of years in many cultures, and in this country they have
become famous for their ability to produce experiences that mimic
those described by Eastern mystics. Huxley's accounts of taking
mescaline are classic descriptions of this, but there are many others;
even the great William James took peyote, but alas he became violently
sick and experienced no mental effects at all — who knows what might
have happened to the science of psychology if he had had a good trip?
More recently, Leary and Alpert began to experiment with LSD, and
the rest of the story is common knowledge. In almost any issue of
Psychedelic Review, for example, one can find an article relating
hallucinogenic experiences to Eastern religion.

The spread of interest in Eastern philosophy in this country,
though it stems from many sources, has been greatly accelerated by
hallucinogen use. It has been not only an effect of LSD experiences but
a cause for more. Five years ago, the hope of a religious or

philosophical revelation was a major reason for taking LSD. Today this has declined, but still a few youths take it hoping for a glimpse of cosmic truth.

But those who really become interested in Eastern philosophy usually go beyond drugs and try an actual discipline – yoga, Zen Buddhism, transcendental meditation, and many others. For example, Bert, the boy who sniffed glue and pounded on his adviser's door, is about to go to Japan to live in a Zen monastery for a year. When I met him a month ago, he told me how it happened:

> Since I got to college, I've done acid a couple of times, not nearly as often as I used to in prep school. It's become more of an incidental thing now. I've sort of lost interest in it. Anyhow, I spent last summer at a sort of Zen summer camp in Rochester, New York, where we did a lot of meditation and heard people talk about Zen. It hasn't revolutionized my life or anything, but I'm definitely going to get deeper into it. I'm in a group now at college that meets every afternoon – I go there three or four times a week – and we meditate for an hour or so. And I'm already starting to make arrangements to take a year off from college and go to Japan in June; I don't think I'll have much trouble getting into a monastery there, from what I've been told. As for drugs, I've really stopped using drugs pretty much. You know, it's not as if I'm trying to force myself to keep from taking them – I just haven't been particularly interested in them. I suppose I'll take LSD again once a year or so, but more for old times' sake than anything else.

As I listened to Bert, it was hard to believe that he had taken LSD scores of times, not to mention DMT, Methedrine, cocaine, opium, and heroin, and yet somehow known all along that drugs did not answer to what he was looking for. They never seemed to interfere with his scholastic or athletic accomplishments and they did not prevent him from entering a prestigious university. Now that he has found a better path to the truth, he has lost interest in them almost entirely.

Another Eastern technique, transcendental meditation as taught by Maharishi Mahesh Yogi, has drawn literally thousands of youths away from drug use; in America, far more than half of its practitioners have used drugs at one time. Since I am myself a transcendental meditator, I have met many former heavy users at meetings and residence courses. Some have abstained completely since they began meditating two or three years ago, but most, like Bert, still use LSD on very rare occasions. Practically none of them has continued to use drugs on a large scale.

It does not follow that one can stop someone from using drugs by encouraging him to meditate: for most of the people I know, the decisions to start meditation and to stop drug use were simultaneous rather than sequential. The step into Eastern philosophy was only part of a general change in life style; it represented not only a new way of looking for enlightenment, but a whole new identity, a whole new answer to the feelings of alienation.

Back to Purity

Some find other alternatives. I have known many users, for example, who became dissatisfied with the feelings of corruption and "impurity" that surrounded drug use. In particular, those who had been using a lot of amphetamines, opiates, or tranquilizers began to feel uncomfortably like some members of the older generation, taking a drug to cure every itch. The idea of pollution began to bother them; while complaining that the Establishment was poisoning the environment, they were daily filling their own bodies with chemicals. Many have decided to return to purity, to join a group doing macrobiotic cooking, go to a commune in the wilderness, or even return to school, usually to study, noncompetitively, some little field that they really care about: zoology, medieval history, or modern music. Often they have worked through some of the feelings that originally led them to drug use, such as anger or loneliness. As for problems that they have not mastered, such as apathy, they have decided that drugs do not help, as in the account of this twenty-year-old boy named Jimmy:

> Well, you know, I've been through drugs. Three years
> ago, I started on grass and that was cool, and then I

got into acid and that was cool, and then for about a year, I was doing lots of acid and grass, and occasionally doing speed and opium, mescaline, a little morphine — you name it. And then after living in that scene for a while, it just got to be a drag, you know, it just wasn't particularly exciting anymore. And I got tired of going to into the dirty kitchen and chasing the cockroaches under the toaster, eating nothing but corn flakes and peanut butter. And so me and this chick I was living with moved into another apartment with three other people and got into macrobiotics. And now I go to bed at ten at night and get up at 6:30 in the morning and eat a really good breakfast of oats or some other grain with honey, and I feel really great all day. It's not as if I purposely stopped taking drugs at any particular time — I just gradually realized that I'd sort of come to the end of the scene, you know, like there just wasn't anything very interesting about it any more. So now I'm getting into a health thing as I said, and I've been doing a lot of reading, and I'm getting into all kinds of things.

Jimmy may not be entirely satisfied with his new life style, but he will probably not return to intensive drug use. I say this more on the basis of experience than on theoretical considerations: I have known a lot of people like him, and they almost never go back to their old ways. This is because the decision to stop using drugs is not an isolated one. As with meditation, it represents a whole change of life style, a broad change not easily reversed.

Drugs and Life Style

Perhaps the most important point of this chapter, if not of the entire section from Lauren's story to Jimmy's, is that drug use is part of an entire life style, reflecting a particular orientation to society and an integrated system of personal values. One cannot understand the origins of drug use without seeing it in the context of the life style surrounding it; this is why much of the previous chapters is devoted to the "scene" as a whole rather than to drug use in particular. And since drug use is not an isolated phenomenon, it occurs in any one individual for a complex of reasons; nobody takes LSD, amphetamines or heroin just for kicks, just to express anger, just to test himself. Psychologically, drug use is never simple.

The reader must also remember that the reasons for taking drugs are at best only partly conscious; most users, particularly younger ones, do not go around deliberately searching for enlightenment or specifically trying to deepen their relationships with other people. Drugs are fun. Why try to explain it? Even college students, who may be capable of sophisticated analyses of the origins of their apathy or loneliness, do not often sit down to formulate their reasons for taking drugs. Naturally, I have quoted those users who did happen to verbalize their feelings well at one time or another and told anecdotes that illustrated a given point with particular clarity. But these are the exceptions; one must bear in mind that in real life, most of the time, this material lies in the unconscious. Drug use is something one *does* rather than analyzes.

This section of the book has described only the reasons for *initial* drug use, the forces which start the process in motion by producing the first few users in a given community or social group. But if twenty students are already taking LSD at high school, it is much easier for the twenty-first to get started than it was for the first two or three; there is already an active subculture, an interpersonal element superimposed on his personal attraction to drugs. In addition to attracting new users, the subculture, assisted by the actual effects of the drugs themselves, tends to perpetuate drug use in all who have joined it. This second stage of the process, the social psychology and pharmacology of drug use, is the subject of the succeeding chapters.

VIII. THE DRUG SUBCULTURE

With a Little Help from My Friends

Recently I saw a billboard which said, "You will want to talk to your children about drugs. Before somebody else does." Who is this "somebody else?" In the minds of many parents, it is the pusher." A lower-class type, older, sinister-looking, addicted to morphine, he issues from his hole in the ghetto and descends upon a virginal suburban high school, eager to expand his clientele. Selecting a gullible-looking sophomore, he whispers, "Hey, man, you wanna buy some pot? It's *you* man! . . . What's the matter? You chicken, huh?"

This story is hogwash. It may happen somewhere, but of dozens of users that I have asked, none has described a scenario even approximating it. In the vast majority of cases, the potential user recieves marijuana from a close friend who is already familiar with its effects. Most users take great pleasure in initiating a novice; the drug is almost always supplied free, together with advice on how to smoke it and how to enjoy the effects. One boy, who has initiated more than ten people, described his feelings as follows:

> I really enjoy turning on somebody to dope for the
> first time. I guess it's partly a power trip thing. You
> know all about it and he doesn't, and it's sort of fun
> to teach him what it's like, to be a father to him. And
> there's a sense of responsibility to it, too. You want
> to be sure he'll have a good time, make sure he's not
> anxious, be careful not to try to force your ideas on
> him as to what you think is good about it. You just
> let him do his thing and get into his own head. Then
> you play him some good rock on a good hi-fi system,
> and he listens for a minute, and his eyes light up, and
> he looks back at you with this look of discovery on
> his face. Suddenly he *knows* why rock sounds this
> way. Suddenly he understands a whole lot of things.
> And that gives me a really cool feeling, to know that
> there's one more person who knows, one more person
> who's begun to see through all the programming he's
> gotten since he was born.

Most users are initiated to drug use through this sort of pleasant
experience, usually with marijuana, occasionally with LSD or
amphetamine. Many not only received the drug free the first time, but
used it with their friends for months before they themselves even
purchased any. Marijuana has always been, to some extent, communal
property: anybody who has some is expected to share it with all who
want a "toke" from the pipe. Eventually, though, a user will want a
supply of his own.

The desire to obtain a supply of a drug becomes one of the first
forces which cause the subculture to form. Users typically begin with
only a few drug-using friends through whom they meet others.
Eventually, they meet a dealer, usually a small-time one, who sells
marijuana by the ounce (about 20-100 doses, costing from $10-$25 in
the East, and half as much in California), and perhaps other drugs,
particularly LSD, other hallucinogens, and amphetamine. Interaction
with the dealer expands the novices' circle of drug-using friends and
tempts them with the immediate possibility of trying other drugs. In
addition, some begin to consider dealing themselves: they have acquired
enough acquaintances to have a market, and they are aware that they

can make sizeable profits, plus an unlimited personal supply, at a modest risk. For example, a boy with as few as fifteen friends, each buying an average of two ounces of marijuana, a little hashish, and two doses of hallucinogens per month, (some of which goes, in turn, to their friends), can earn $100 a week with very little effort.

But for most dealers, money is only of secondary importance. They enjoy the thrill of being involved in a dangerous business, the challenge of outwitting the police, and the admiration of their clients: dealing is a reaction to the "sheltered life" already described. This attitude is revealed in their accounts:

> Sure it's dangerous, and sometimes I lose money or give the stuff away, so it's not really that profitable. But there's something really cool about putting through a big deal and almost getting busted by the feds. It takes guts, sometimes.

Another dealer expressed more vividly the idea of proving himself:

> The narks already have my name. I know they have. Maybe they'll bust me soon. But to eighty people in this little town, I'm looked up to as *the man.* They depend on me for their grass and acid. There's something I really like about sticking with it, never quite getting caught. It's all a game, man, I admit – sometimes it's a real ego thing, but it's fun.

A big dealer named Ken, at a prestigious university, described a large-scale deal:

> One of the most educational experiences in my whole college career was when I did a transcontinental gram of acid, four thousand doses. Three of us got together and each put in $900, and we went up to see "acid man" in New York. He flew to the Coast and picked it up in San Francisco. I can remember sitting in that little apartment on the Lower East Side when he came in with one little vial of orange powder. It looked so tiny – it was hard to believe that it was worth three thousand dollars. We each dropped about a tenth of a match head worth of it and got zonked out of our minds for about ten hours. It was the purest, most beautiful acid I've ever seen. It was a

tense scene though. We had two other guys with us, one of whom was an expert at Karate and the other armed with tear gas guns, just in case someone tried to rip us off. And have you ever seen $2700 in fives and tens? It was a heavy scene, man, *extremely* heavy. But anyhow, we drove it back down to school, and spent all night capping it. Even the dust in the air was enough to make us start tripping again. But we capped it into two thousand caps and sold it for the next two months.

You know, I didn't really earn a tremendous amount of money off that deal. I gave it away to all my friends, and sold some in quantity at only a very small profit. Perhaps I made seven hundred dollars, but I could have made the same amount in less time in legal ways. But that deal and the incidents surrounding it really taught me a lot. It was a really exhilarating experience to have done it. I may try to do it again sometime. And when I'm a dottering eighty-year-old grandfather and my grandchildren are sitting on my knee, I'll be able to say, "Kids, did I ever tell you about the good old days, when LSD was still illegal, when I did a transcontinental gram?"

Ken did try to do it again. Perhaps if he had been able to find a different adventure to test his competence, he would not now be in jail.

Having Fought in the War

Even if one never becomes involved in dealing, the step into illegality is crucial: as in all deviant subcultures, the need for secrecy binds heavy users together. Sharing experiences that most people have not known, they develop an *esprit de corps* which increases with deepening involvement in drugs. Fraternity is constantly reinforced by common jargon, styles of dress, dozens of little rituals, and by the exchange of frightening stories about the activity of those on the other side: the feds, the fuzz, and the narks. Such stories range from absolute truth to classical paranoia. An example near the latter end of the spectrum is this account from a big dealer, himself a heavy user of hallucinogens, in New York:

"My partner arrived from the Coast with a gram and I was doing a two-building thing – you know, keeping the stuff in one building and selling it out of another. Well, this car from the CIA came driving up the road. . . ."

"How did you know it was from the CIA?"

"Of course it was from the CIA. I overheard the conversation of the two cats who got out of the car. One of them was from the CIA and the other was some federal agent from New York. Anyhow, they were talking about someone dealing acid, and then one man got back in the car and the other stayed there."

"Why would the CIA be interested in getting someone for dealing acid? Are you sure they were not just regular narcotics agents?"

"No, man, don't you see? The CIA is part of the government, right? And the people in the government know that if too many people get turned on to acid, they'll start seeing through the whole thing. They'll start seeing through all the government's schemes and revolt. And so the government has the CIA working in this country to get all the acid dealers it can."

"What happened?"

"Well, anyhow, this cat walked around outside my apartment for awhile and then he turned and walked toward the door. I had about 750 doses left and I flushed them all down the toilet. Just as I got through doing it, we heard a pounding on the door, and we all escaped out the back door of the apartment."

Though not always so fantastic, accounts such as this are common among drug users. I have heard some stories about the American Legion dropping thumb tacks on Boston Common in the knowledge that most of the street people were barefoot, about the Mafia putting rat poison and animal tranquilizers into all the marijuana in town, about the police mercilessly shooting three long-haired teenagers in a small California town. Even if these stories were false – and not all of them are – they sounded quite convincing when they were told to me. In combination with the very real dangers of illegality, they provide a powerful unifying force for drug users.

Users feel that theirs is an "in-group;" outsiders have not experienced what they have. As one boy described it:

> You know how guys who have both fought in France in World War I talk to each other about old times? The feeling that they've had a really special experience, that they've got a special bond between them, a common memory that sets them a little apart from other slobs. Well, maybe when we are sitting around in the old folk's home, we'll reminisce about our acid trips, and the deals we put through, and the times we almost got busted when we were young.

Many users felt that they entered the "in-group" when they first experienced LSD; they now understood what it was all about, they realized why the effects could not be described in words, and they suddenly could communicate with others who had taken hallucinogens. And even those who were not so impressed, who did not feel such a dramatic transformation, still recognized, at some level in their minds, that their "eyes had seen the glory," that they had a new basis for fraternity with other users.

In some areas of the country, where drug use is still uncommon, even the first marijuana experience can produce the "in-group" feeling. I remember a Harvard student's account of the morning after his first high in 1966. This story would sound ridiculous for a Cambridge user in the seventies, but it probably still would apply in many areas of the country.

> I felt bouncy as I walked down the street. I looked around at all the adults and somehow I felt special, above all of them. I knew where it was at, man! I knew that grass was not dangerous the way they thought it was. After awhile I walked into a store and bought a paisley shirt. It was all I needed, I was the *compleat* hippy. I smiled at a long-haired guy as he passed on the street. It was as if somehow, he could automatically recognize that I had smoked grass.

There is some truth in the last sentence of this story: one heavy user can identify another, even if he has short hair and ordinary dress, through a few gestures and the exchange of a few sentences. Once the exchange is completed, the two are almost friends. It is impossible to specify on paper the elements of such an interaction; the proper jargon is most important, but it must be used and pronounced in the right way and coupled with little gestures and details of behavior of which one is hardly aware. For example, I once passed two boys on Charles Street in Boston. One had just asked the other if there was any hashish available.

> "Too bad you weren't here a couple of weeks ago. There was some *beautiful* hash going around then," I said.

They looked at me with suspicion because my hair was too short and perhaps they detected a bit of straightness in my accent or my manner.

> "I'm not putting you on, man. Two tokes and you were zonked out of your mind. It cost a dime for sort of a short gram, but was really worth it. It's all been smoked up by now."

We talked for about five minutes more. By the end, they were confident that I was OK, and one gave me a "V" sign with his fingers as he went away.

> "Take care!" I said. He smiled back.

Of course I did not always establish rapport so quickly, but most of the time, all that was needed was a knowledge of the jargon and of the effects of the drugs. In this encounter, as in many others, drugs provided an immediate topic for conversation and a means of quickly making friends.

These examples I hope give some idea of the "feel" of the drug subculture — of the powerful fraternity which common experience and common danger confer on its members. It is exciting and gratifying, a defense against loneliness; in a word, it is an identity for youths who have been searching for one for a long time. To many it is more attractive even than the effects of the drugs themselves.

Reference Group and Self-Image

Behind the easily demonstrable effects of supply, secrecy, and common experience, more subtle forces draw the user into the subculture. One of these is the need for approval and reassurance from his reference group — the group by whose values he measures himself — which comes to include a larger and larger proportion of users. Within a few months of their first drug experiences, most of the users I have known began to associate more with other users and to draw away from their straight friends who did not approve of drugs. A high school girl described this as follows:

> It was just too much of a hassle to explain it to some of my friends in high school. They were really immature, still afraid to think for themselves about drugs. Many of them knew that marijuana was safe, but I think basically they were scared. Anyhow, many of them sort of disapproved of using drugs, and it was a drag to be around them. There were only about twenty of us who were really into drugs then, although there are many more now, and we used to get together in little groups after school.

I do not think that this girl, whom I knew very well, felt any guilt in the presence of her straight friends; it was simply unpleasant for her to deal with their air of disapproval.

The youth who becomes deeply involved with heavier drugs, such as LSD, amphetamines, or heroin, selects friends who not only approve of drug use, but reassure him that it is relatively safe. This is caused by "cognitive dissonance": as the cigarette smoker does not want to hear about lung cancer, and the social drinker dislikes being preached to about the evils of alcohol addiction, so the speed freak does not relish the thought of his dying brain cells, nor the LSD user entertain the idea that he might go psychotic. The more dangerous the drug, the more the user will select as his friends people who de-emphasize or deny the dangers. Indeed, the LSD group will often go as far as to reverse the situation by defining the undesirable effects as valuable and enlightening experiences. A heavy LSD user on the Lower East Side was very emphatic about this:

Of course you're going to have some freaky experiences after you've taken a few heavy trips. And sure some of them are going to be really frightening. But they're important. They accelerate the process of learning about yourself that LSD has started. If you get scared and go back into your hole just because you suddenly notice that you feel a little strange every day, or the world suddenly looks different, you're not going to get anywhere. When the things that are all cooped up inside you start coming out, man, it's not all going to be rosy. I mean, you've got to learn that everybody has things like this inside them, and when you have some bad experiences after your last acid trip, it may be the best thing that ever happened to you.

Among the street people, approval and acceptance of LSD aftereffects is only a specific case of a general tolerance for all forms of unconventional behavior and strange experiences. Some of this represents a reaction formation to prejudices which they have perceived in the older generation: they react with sympathy and friendship, rather than disgust or avoidance, to a drunk on a park bench, a heroin addict, a draft dodger hiding from the law, or a homosexual harrassed by the police. Tolerance also results from what I have called psychological sophistication: users believe that acting out is desirable, that it is a way of expressing one's real self and escaping from the arbitrary restrictions of a sick society. As a result, the subculture attracts to itself many kinds of social deviants other than drug users, who value the relaxed, "do your own thing" atmosphere, the relief from disapproval and criticism that it provides.

Paralleling increasing social involvement with the subculture — and continued exposure to its tolerance and approval — are changes on a cognitive level, a reorientation of one's values and self-image. For most users I have known, these changes were so gradual as to go almost unnoticed; most have had the experience of looking back a year or two and suddenly realizing with some surprise, and even pride, how far they had come. One of the street people in Boston, a boy of seventeen, described this:

> You know, two years ago I thought dope was something like heroin. It was associated in my mind with junkies shooting up skag in Harlem and dying from an overdose. I didn't even know a single person who had done grass — God, that's hard to believe — and it was completely inconceivable to me that I would even try any. God, I've come a long way since then — I was so incredibly naive in those days, I just didn't know what was coming off at all. Now it's sort of hard to imagine what it even feels like *not* to have smoked dope.

Initially, such changes in thought have little relation to the physiological aftereffects of the drugs themselves; they are the product of a gradual shift in reference group and of greater experience with drug effects. Greater familiarity with the drugs and the subculture breeds a progressively more relaxed attitude towards bigger drugs and possible dangers.

For heavy users, drug use ultimately becomes what Becker has called a "master trait" — the central fact of personality by which self-image and behavior are defined. This is because drugs absorb most of the user's time and conversation, and perhaps because this is how he is perceived by the outside world, as a member of a homogeneous, almost faceless group defined primarily by the fact that it uses drugs of various kinds. Once he has defined himself and is defined by others as a "head," it is hard to break away from the label. I have known many people who have ceased to use LSD or even drugs as a whole. But months or even years after their last trip, their circle of friends still includes a large fraction of drug users, and they still may consider themselves to be members of the subculture.

Finally, drug use may develop into not only a master trait, but a measure of one's status within the subculture. Those who have used LSD most or who have had the widest experience with different drugs are often leaders of their circles. Many times I have heard less experienced users ask them for descriptions of their experiences with more exotic drugs, or advice on how best to enjoy an LSD trip.

In these ways, the subculture can completely reverse the qualms of potential users. As they become more and more involved with a reference group that approves of and encourages drug experiences, and as they begin to label themselves and be labeled as "heads," drug use rises from a curiosity to a master trait, from an image of corruption and degradation to a status symbol.

The Media

The subculture derives much of its unity from its status of opposition to the Establishment. But, like other deviant subcultures, it is simultaneously strengthened by a contrapuntal note of *approval* in society, particularly through the media. As with "bikies" or gangsters, American society officially condemns drug users on one hand but romanticizes them on the other — in movies, on television, in magazines, in the newspapers, and, of course, in music. A college friend named Jim described this for the case of Woodstock:

> "I went to Woodstock, and spent six hours stuck in the traffic jam, and then got there and got covered with mud, and got rained on, and got sick, and didn't get much to eat, and didn't even hear too much music. There were good things about it, but basically it was really an ordeal. So afterwards we drove home, and again got stuck in the traffic jam, and finally got back to Boston. So then I picked up a magazine and read about what a wonderful time I had had, and how it had been a huge festival of life, and filled with good vibes, and love, and great music, and so on. Sure, a lot of people enjoyed it a good deal, and I'm glad it happened, but the media played it up incredibly — they made it into a much more beautiful scene than it really was, and made it look like it was a really loving and cool thing. The media do that a lot of the time, and they give kids the idea that there are all kinds of beautiful things waiting for them if they get into the scene."

> "But don't you think that the media exaggerate equally in the other direction, too?"

> "Well, sure, they play up the cases where some kid dies of an o.d. of heroin, and once in a while they go into a thing about the dangers of dope. But the kids *know* that dope isn't dangerous, and they're pretty

sure they won't end up o.d'ing on skag, so they don't
fall for that part. Instead they believe all the good
parts — they really eat up the stuff about how groovy
a scene Woodstock was, and they decide that they
want to get in on it."

"That's true, I think, but why do kids believe the
positive things so easily?"

"I don't know. For one thing, they *want* to believe
the positive parts. And then, another thing that I
think of that's probably really important: the media
are written more for adults — and the media are
constantly looking for things that whet the appetites
of adults, things that will sell, you know? And the
adults I know just eat up the stuff they read about
Woodstock, and they go to see the movie to see the
kids skinny dipping, and rolling in the mud, and being
happy. The media like to emphasize things like that
because they know that's what sells, that that's what
turns on the people who read it. And so naturally
when the kids get pelted with all of this stuff, they
decide it must be true."

The movie "Hippie Love-In," mentioned earlier, is a more blatant
example of the same phenomenon that Jim described for Woodstock:
the media offer a vicarious satisfaction to those who, though sincerely
disapproving of the drug culture, are fascinated by it. While catering to
this interest in the older generation, the media inevitably encourage the
younger.

The media also help to raise the subculture to a national and
international level. High school students in an isolated city in the
Midwest or South learn that they are not alone, that youths all over the
country, and in Canada and Europe, are taking LSD, amphetamine, and
heroin: the local reference group is reinforced by its alliance with drug
users all over the world. A particularly striking case of this was
described by a boy from Philadelphia:

A little while ago, there was an article about drug use
among younger kids in some magazine. The article
had a photograph of a bunch of fifth or sixth graders
sitting around smoking dope. The picture was
probably simulated — probably none of the kids in

the picture had even *seen* any dope. But the effect of
that picture was that sixth graders all around the
country looked at that article and said, "Gosh, I'm
really getting behind. Here I am turning twelve years
old and I haven't even smoked *dope* yet!" And so of
course he smokes dope a lot sooner than as if he'd
never seen that picture. I know personally two
seventh graders who started doing dope just because
they had seen that article. Of course the article said in
words, "Isn't this terrible, all these little kids doing
dope," but on another level it was saying, "Hey, kid,
this is where it's at. It's time that you get with it."
And of course the kids responded to that level.

I heard relatively few accounts like this in 1968, but I cannot
count the number that I have heard in 1970 and 1971: drug users are
increasingly aware of the catalytic effect of the media on the growth of
their subculture. Drug use would probably have slowly spread across
the country without the media, but only with their reinforcement
could it have so explosively spread from a few small nuclei to a national
scale.

Thus the subculture acquires its unity in response to both the
obvious opposition and the subtle support of the Establishment. For
the heavy user, involvement in the subculture is usually the result of a
long succession of individual steps, beginning perhaps with reading
magazine articles, watching television, listening to rock music, and
talking to those already in the subculture. Then he is introduced to
drug use through a few friends, followed perhaps by some interaction
with a dealer, then a growing feeling of unity with the "in-group " that
is reinforced by the rituals and jargon of the subculture and the
excitement of being outside of the law and society. For a few the
process is rapid, but for most, it is a slow education in the attitudes and
values of users, a gradual change in self-image, the result of the
progressive replacement of the voices of the outside world with those
from within the subculture.

IX. MARIJUANA AND THE HALLUCINOGENS

Drug Effects

The psychotropic, or mind-affecting drugs used by American youths can be roughly divided into three categories: marijuana and the hallucinogens, the "stimulants," such as amphetamine, methamphetamine, and cocaine, and the "depressants," such as alcohol, barbiturates, opiates, and their relatives. Chapters IX-XI deal with the pharmacological effects and long-term aftereffects of each class of drugs, but only insofar as they contribute to the actual formation and perpetuation of the subculture: this does not constitute a review of their pharmacology. It is tempting, for instance, to debate the effect of LSD on chromosomes, but such material, though important, will be mentioned only when it is specifically relevant to the actual use of drugs. The reader who wishes to pursue such questions in the pharmacological literature can find appropriate references at the end of the book.

Unfortunately, some of the medical facts most relevant to the social psychology of drug use cannot be found in the literature: certain questions, difficult to answer in the laboratory or the clinic, are best explored in the field. In such cases, I have relied on my own observations of several thousand instances of drug use in a vast variety of social settings. As in the earlier chapters, my conclusions, unless otherwise noted, are based on these observations.

Marijuana

Marijuana is the name for the dried leaves, tops, seeds, and stems of the female *Cannabis Sativa* plant, most of which is brought into this country from Mexico, Central America, North Africa, India, and Vietnam. Many users grow their own in the United States – on the front porch, in the living room window, under a fluorescent light in the cellar, or even by the acre in the southern parts of the country. Marijuana is known as "grass" to old-timers, and "dope" to modern users; anyone who consistently refers to it as "pot" will establish himself as an outsider to the subculture. The crushed tops of the plant are available separately as "kief", and the pure resin from the leaves, called hashish or "hash", comes from North Africa, the Middle East, and Kashmir. Supposedly the active principle of marijuana, tetrahydrocannabinol, or THC, is also available to users, but this is unlikely, since THC is difficult to synthesize or extract. Most, if not all, of the capsules which dealers offer as "THC" might be in fact LSD, other hallucinogens, tranquilizers, or nothing but crushed aspirin tablets.

The effects of marijuana, kief and hashish are all similar, differing mainly in degree: twenty lungfuls of mediocre marijuana are equivalent to five lungfuls of a better grade, and two of kief or hashish. The effects are usually pleasant: they are rather like an intermediate state between sleep and wakefulness. Varied images, more vivid than ordinary thought but less real than dreams, rush rapidly through the mind. Emotions are usually intensified – one laughs at the smallest joke and cries at even a slightly sentimental movie. Music of all forms becomes fascinating to listen to; one is conscious of hundreds of little details one had not noticed before. Food tastes much better than usual, and sexual experiences, most users would agree, are enhanced, although the drug does not appear to directly stimulate sexual functions in any way. After an hour or two, the sedative effects begin to dominate the other sensations, and one is content to quietly listen to music or even fall asleep. Marijuana almost always produces this picture of mild sedation: rarely do users become more active under its influence. Of the 500 to 1500 people whom I have seen intoxicated with marijuana, none has ever displayed increased violent or aggressive behavior.

For these reasons, most users, particularly those who are experienced with marijuana, are astonished by the Establishment's reaction to it. To the experienced smoker, marijuana seems quieting, rather mild, sometimes amusing, usually trivial, and often downright dull. But society defines what he considers a commonplace and harmless act as deviant, dangerous, and illegal, carrying jail sentences comparable to grand larceny and second-degree murder. He does not constantly ruminate about this, of course, but it always exists, in the back of his mind, as a reservoir for anger and suspicion, a basis for doubting the validity of many other laws and attitudes. He perceives it as one of the most absolutely unequivocal cases in which society is wrong and he is right, as a clear demonstration that he knows more about drugs than his parents and teachers and is therefore better qualified than they to dictate which ones he shall use and how often. He sees the older generation's hostility towards marijuana as a display of ignorance, of hypocrisy, and perhaps of thinly disguised envy. He reacts with a stronger alliance to the subculture, a more rapid acceptance of its beliefs, and often, the use of bigger drugs. From the standpoint of social psychology, the effects or dangers of marijuana are secondary; it is the fact that *it is widely defined as deviant* that gives marijuana overwhelming importance as one of the solid foundations of the subculture in America.

Many users quoted in Chapter V displayed this hostility about the illegality of marijuana. Some examples are users who tried marijuana, then angrily concluded that their parents and teachers had been "lying" about its dangers, and therefore ceased to believe any warnings about other drugs. Some have tried bigger drugs partially to express this anger, and many have sensed envy behind the hostility of the Establishment. Two other particularly vivid accounts from marijuana users further illustrate their feelings. The first is from Eliot, the college dropout quoted at length in Chapter III:

> Does marijuana lead to heroin? Yes, in a sense. *I* would never have tried heroin if I had not first used marijuana. *Why* does marijuana lead to heroin? The *effects* of marijuana don't lead to heroin. Alcohol is vastly more similar to heroin than grass. The person who enjoys the effects of alcohol is much more likely to like heroin than the person who enjoys the effects of grass. So the chemistry of marijuana does not lead to heroin. But the illegality of marijuana does, or at least it certainly did for me. Because once I had taken that step across the line by trying grass, a lot of my ideas changed. First I recognized that I could get away with something illegal, and that the fact that it was illegal made it much more fun. It's just like if women went around topless, we wouldn't get nearly so turned on by their breasts. Also, I learned that illegal things were not bad for you — it was perfectly obvious to me, as it is to every other smoker, that the laws against marijuana are unjustified. So I learned from the marijuana laws that laws were often evil and that even if they were right, that you could break them with nil chance of getting caught. And suddenly the possibility of heroin seemed a lot less remote. Six months later, just for amusement, I shot up heroin. It was sort of fun. I'll do it again someday. So for me and I think for a lot of other guys, marijuana itself doesn't lead to heroin. The law leads to heroin! The Marijuana Tax Act, by transforming an innocent intoxicant into a school for crime, has coaxed thousands of innocent kids down the road to heroin.

The other account is from the medical student quoted near the beginning of Chapter III:

> Our society practically applauds alcohol, a drug that directly or indirectly accounts for 5% of all deaths every year, and that's conservative. It kills brain cells, leads to psychoses, rots your liver, kills thousands of drivers, and of course is seriously addictive. Its social and emotional toll in broken families and ruined lives

is incalculable. Now your average dope smoker may not know all the statistics, but he knows enough to be absolutely sure that alcohol is more dangerous than dope and the fact that booze is legal and dope isn't stands as a monument of hypocrisy in our culture. It gives the dope user a little taste of what it feels like to be arbitrarily discriminated against. It gives him just a faint idea of what it must feel like to be black, for instance — to have some big, powerful people tell you that you can't do something just because it doesn't appeal to them.

Perhaps not all of these statements are valid, but they are certainly representative of the views of marijuana users. Most would not express their ideas as forcefully or as eloquently, but even the youngest smoker shares a little of the same bitterness.

Returning to pharmacology, do "panic reactions" to marijuana have any role in the formation of the subculture? If they do, it is certainly minor: in the thousands of cases of marijuana or hashish intoxication I have witnessed, I have seen only two instances of severe panic, both of which lasted less than an hour. However, mild anxiety, called "paranoia" by most users, is not uncommon. Practically all experienced smokers can recall some occasions on which they had unrealistic fears of getting arrested or being noticed by other people. Since the presence of friends usually minimizes paranoia, users are drawn together.

What is the role of long-term aftereffects of marijuana? I have never met a user *of marijuana and hashish alone* who described, or displayed, any recognizable long term aftereffects. At most, users feel sluggish the day after smoking heavily, and very rarely they may feel slightly dazed for as much as a week after the last dose. In particular, I can remember a single batch of "Acapulco Gold" that produced this effect in seven different people who smoked it. All of them were quite surprised, for they had never in the past experienced comparable aftereffects from marijuana.

The aftereffects of marijuana, then, do not seem to have much effect on the subculture. The heavy smoker may feel sleepy much of the time, and possibly this augments his pre-existing apathy towards the outside world. Beyond this, not much can be explained on the basis of marijuana or hashish effects alone. But LSD is another story.

The Big Hallucinogens: Communication

Much has already been said about the effects of LSD and why a knowledge of these effects leads a youth initially to try it; it is a relief from boredom, an enhancement of sentience, a source of fusion, an escape from the sheltered life, an initiation, a way to express anger or withdrawal, an answer to loneliness, a substitute for sex, a moving psychological, philosophical, or religious experience, and, most importantly, it is fun. These factors also help to perpetuate use beyond the first trip: hallucinogen use can become an identity which buffers against the discontents of alienation, a basis for one's social life, or even, for the intellectual user, a continuing psychological or philosophical quest. In the previous chapter, we have seen further ways in which drug use in general can bring users together into a subculture, which in turn acts to perpetuate use. But there is more to be said about the specific case of the hallucinogens: certain effects and aftereffects unique to this class of chemicals are particularly important in the formation and perpetuation of the subculture and the drug use within it.

First, LSD, unlike marijuana or alcohol, is frequently unpleasant when one is alone, for this greatly increases the risk of a bad trip, or, as it is more graphically called, a "horror show." Imagine, for example, this experience of a college student from Colorado who spent four hours of his first trip alone in his room, recording his impressions onto a tape recorder:

> The fear kept building up and I couldn't fight it. There was no one I could reference myself against, no one to ask whether something was real or in my imagination. It got so that I did not even dare to move from my tape recorder. It was the only reality and I was connected to reality by the thin cable of the microphone. I could not imagine what might happen to me if suddenly the microphone plug pulled out of the back of the machine. Maybe the whole

world would just melt away in front of my eyes. I wanted to go to the bathroom, but I was afraid that if I did I would see something coming up behind me in the mirror. Or maybe while I was standing there, my image would grin at me and turn and walk away. I thought, "If something happens, I can always scream and one of my roommates will wake up and help me." But then I thought, "What if my mind decides, just for its own amusement, not to let me scream?"

At one point, I stood up from the tape recorder on the floor, and there was this *thing*, crouching behind the bookcase, waiting to get me. It looked vaguely human, but it was made of light and it vanished when I looked straight at it. But I did a backwards standing broad jump of about five feet and stood with my back against the wall, surveying the whole room and saying out loud, "Now I can see the whole room and nothing can sneak up on me!" And just as I said it I felt a hand, real as life, stroking the back of my neck. Somehow I convinced myself that the hand wasn't real and ran to the telephone, called a friend, and he got out of bed and came over. I was so relieved to see him that I embraced him and cried. After that, everything was groovy — not a trace of fear. Since that time, I've never tripped alone, and all my trips have been just beautiful. Nothing brings out your need for another human being like an acid trip.

It is not surprising that one such experience would lead a user to seek friends to accompany him on subsequent trips. Not only do friends protect each other from horror shows, but as already described, communication while tripping can sometimes be a moving emotional experience. Some users go so far as to believe that LSD can confer telepathic powers; I have never witnessed this, but there is no doubt that many users derive from it a sense of deep nonverbal communication with one another.

Another significant form of communication is the exchange of accounts of past experiences. This is unimportant in most other drug subcultures — alcohol, heroin, or amphetamine produces roughly the same effects every time; users do not spend much time recounting the actual mental phenomena that they have experienced. But past hallucinogen experiences provide a vast resevoir for anecdotes and conversations. The exchange of accounts between experienced users serves as a way of passing time and establishing rapport. In particular, it is a frequent topic of conversation between users who have recently met: a way of demonstrating to one another that they "know where it's at" — that they are experienced members of the subculture. The following conversations among three users who had just met is not merely an interesting description of effects, but a good example of this important mechanism for establishing rapport:

> "Psilocybin? Man, that's the freakiest thing I've ever done. I've only done it twice, but the first time, I went out for a walk and I met this really nice man on a street corner. He'd never tripped or anything, but he was fairly hip, you know, and I'd been talking to him for about half an hour — half an hour — and suddenly it occurred to me that he didn't exist, that I had hallucinated him. And then I realized that I wasn't on a street corner at all, but in my room sitting on my bed, smoking a non-existent cigarette out of a non-existent package of Marlboros!"

> "Yeah, that's really freaky stuff. I've never done psilocybin. Even on the really big doses of acid, I've always been able to distinguish reality. I always knew where I was."

> "I've got a friend who tried a big dose of psilocybin and he was sitting on his couch in his room, hallucinating a whole cocktail party going on in his room! Just an exquisitely detailed hallucination — he could see every detail on everybody's face. And he turned to his roommate and said, 'Hey, this psilocybin is really freaky stuff! I'm hallucinating a whole cocktail party that doesn't exist!' And the roommate replied, 'That's nothing. I don't exist either!' At which point, the whole cocktail party, *and* the roommate vanished, leaving this guy sitting alone on his couch."

> "Yeah, another one that's really heavy like that is belladonna. You ever done belladonna?"

> "Yes, and I'll never do it again. It was a real bummer. I reached my hand in a wastebasket and there were these rats and cockroaches crawling all over my hand and eating my skin and everything. Jesus, man, it was

the most frightening trip I've ever had!"

The Big Hallucinogens: The Aftereffects

The aftereffects of LSD and its relatives fall roughly into the two catagories of "physical" and "psychological." In the first category, only the reports of chromosome damage have influenced users or potential users. A few have been scared away from LSD by these reports, but the vast majority are aware that other scientists have reported no chromosome damage, or that aspirin, caffeine, and other drugs have been shown to produce similar damage. Many more educated users regard the chromosome reports as an irresponsible scare-story from the scientific world, a case in which the opponents of drugs have cried "wolf" once too often. The others simply ignore the reports entirely.

Among the psychological aftereffects of LSD, perhaps the most famous are the "flashbacks," in which the full effects spontaneously return for about half an hour, sometimes weeks or even months after the last trip. Though relatively rare, these are often cited as one of the dangers of LSD, as indeed they can be, if one happens to be driving down the turnpike at eighty miles per hour and the headlights of approaching cars suddenly turn into a barrage of color. But many users, with the support of their reference group, enjoy flashbacks: as one said, "It's like getting a trip free!" In some circles, it is almost a status symbol to have flashbacks; it marks a user as a true head, one who has really "gotten into acid." This is a fine example of how the subculture can allay the fears of its members – a possible liability of LSD is redefined as an asset.

By far the most important hallucinogen aftereffect, in terms of its influence on the subculture, is that of prolonged "psychotic" symptoms. Among infrequent users, these are quite uncommon, and when they do occur, usually unworthy of being called "psychotic," as some examples will show. The first two stories are from veterans of about fifteen trips over the course of a year or more:

> I was trying to cross Massachusetts Avenue two days
> after tripping, and I kept noticing things flickering in

the corner of my eyes. It was sort of a nuisance, but no more than that.

I took a high school exam three days after that 1000-mike trip. When I looked at the exam I felt really confident. I knew all the answers. I did the whole exam in about half the period and walked out feeling sure that I'd gotten an A or at worst a B⁺. When I got the exam back a week later, it was a D, and when I looked it over, I realized that I really had not known a lot of answers.

These last two occurred after a single trip:

For about a week I couldn't walk through the lobby of A-entry at the dorm without getting really scared, because of the goblin I saw there when I was tripping.

For a month after my first trip I had this weird hangup that my mind would get up and run away from me, that I'd suddenly go insane while walking down the street. Then one day I realized that that was ridiculous, and I haven't worried about it since.

The following account, from a student who took LSD three times in a month, is one of the rare cases of frank psychotic aftereffects in a light user:

I felt sort of disoriented for about a month after my last trip. And then one day I glanced up at the window, and for just an instant, there was a face, real as life, looking in the window at me. Scared me out of my mind. But it's been six months since that time, and nothing like it has happened again.

This boy, not surprisingly, abstained from hallucinogens for a long time after seeing the face in the window. But he is the exception: of the users I have known who tripped less than once a month, only one or two in a hundred ceased to use hallucinogens primarily because of alarming aftereffects.

Among youths who take hallucinogens more often than once a month, the incidence of aftereffects is considerably higher. Of those who have used LSD several times a week for a long period, practically all have experienced striking changes in their thoughts and perceptions.

For example, a heavy LSD user in Pennsylvania once arrived at a dance wearing two pairs of pants. Someone asked him for an explanation, and he said:

> Well, when I was getting dressed for the dance I opened my closet and all my clothes were flying around saying, "Wear me! Wear me!" and then these two pairs of pants got into an incredible fight with each other about which one would be allowed to be worn, so finally I settled the argument by deciding to wear both of them, and that way they were satisfied.

Another heavy user, about a week after his most recent trip, looked up at the sky and said to me:

> I can see all kinds of big cracks in the sky. There are all these cracks forming, and some of the stars are falling out of their places, and light, purple light, is shining through the cracks. I know it isn't real, but I like it — it's sort of beautiful.

These are somewhat extreme cases, but not far removed from the everyday experience of many heavy users. Why are they not disturbed by this? Why do they accept such symptoms and continue to use hallucinogens?

The process of accepting hallucinogen aftereffects is similar to the progress of some cases of schizophrenia. In the first stage of schizophrenia, the individual is alarmed by the symptoms and attempts to hide them from other people. This is followed by a second stage of acceptance of the symptoms and more overt schizophrenic behavior. He may describe the transition between the stages as a moment of revelation, a sudden realization that "everything was all right after all." A schizophrenic friend of mine, who has never taken a hallucinogen, was perhaps describing such a moment in this account:

> For months I had been feeling sort of numb and confused. Nothing seemed to have any meaning. I didn't know where I was or what I was doing or what was going on around me. Then, one night, when I was sitting in a little Indian restaurant, I had a sudden, incredible rush of euphoria. All in an instant everything fell into place and I suddenly realized that

> I had attained a new level of understanding. I rushed
> out of the restaurant laughing. Since then I've found
> that I can accomplish anything I desire, know
> anything I want to know. I know more about
> philosophy than anybody in the philosophy
> department in the university, more about math than
> anyone in the math department, more about English
> than anyone in the English department. I can speak
> any language I wish.

Hallucinogen aftereffects are usually very different from "real" schizophrenia; this discussion is *not* to imply that they are the same. But a similar two-stage process of acceptance seems to occur, although the moment of revelation may not be so abrupt. At first the user is alarmed by the aftereffects; he tries to fight them or deny them, or he decreases the frequency of his trips. Here the subculture plays an enormously important role: it provides a gentle pressure to continue using hallucinogens frequently, a constant subtle insistence that the aftereffects are not bad, that he should not only accept them, but redefine them as desirable. Every time that he becomes alarmed, during a trip or afterwards, other users respond with the oldest, most classic line of advice in the LSD-world, "Don't fight it."

Gradually, in response to the advice of his peers and with the help of the aftereffects themselves, the user passes from the rough first stage into the smooth stage beyond. Suddenly everything is all right — he feels that he has attained new insight, new capacities, a new way of looking at the world. He may recognize that he has lost some of his ability to cope with the complexities of our society, but this seems more than compensated by his enhanced spiritual awareness. This was described by one girl who had taken LSD, mescaline, psilocybin, STP, MDA, TMA, DMT, DET, and other hallucinogens a total of about 500 times:

> Oh no, I don't worry about any "aftereffects" as you
> call them. Long ago they used to bother me a lot.
> When I felt really freaked out, I would stop doing
> acid for a month or two. But after I'd been down
> here a couple of weeks, I realized that I was still a
> victim of the Establishment's definitions of how to
> think and that acid is really where it's at. I looked

back and realized that I had come a long way from where I was before. You have to learn not to fight the truth, but to let it come in, to groove on it. Now I'm a hundred times wiser and more alive than I ever was before. My mind works much better. I can understand the way in which the whole universe works in a way that I never could before. And I'm doing many more things. I'm not stagnating around like I used to. I have all kinds of things I want to get into.

I am also reminded of a boy who was trying to induce me to become a head myself:

After your exams are over, you've got to start with two or three really big trips — a couple of thousand mikes. It takes awhile to really get into it, but if you take a lot of it the first few times, it's much better.

I have heard this advice several times. It may be that a few big doses, spaced at short intervals, are more likely to carry one rapidly through the rough first stage to the point of acceptance.

The behavior of the group that has accepted the aftereffects is different from that of any other I have known. Its members have a remarkable openness and automatic friendliness, a natural ingenuous quality that I have rarely seen in people. When I first met them, my impression was that this was wonderful, the way all people ought to be. I felt very comfortable among them and responded as warmly as I could. But gradually a second impression emerged: many revealed a sort of inconsiderateness, an inability to comprehend and account for other people. There was never malice in this; it was simply as though the others did not exist. For instance, I can remember half a dozen acid-heads who regularly spoke so softly that it was impossible to hear them from more than two feet away. Even when I asked them to speak more loudly, they would quickly revert to their original tone. Another example: many could not understand me if I refused to take LSD with them. No matter how many times I declined, they had forgotten it an hour later and I would have to explain again. Some were remarkably dishonest while remaining warm and friendly. A boy in California told me that a close friend of his had once stolen $20 worth of marijuana from him and seemed surprised when he demanded it back. In a word, many heavy users seem "childish," both in positive and negative senses. To use an old phrase the "flower children" have the wonderful spontaneity and friendliness of children, a capacity to have fun, and a refreshing freedom from sober intellectualization, but also the child's rapidly fluctuating moods and difficulty with long term, responsible interpersonal relationships.

Looking deeper, it appears that many acid-heads shift from ordinary neurotic defenses against reality to a denial of reality when it does not suit them. In a sense, LSD seems to "cure" neurosis by substituting psychosis. Primary process thought begins to dominate over secondary process; fantasy in general, and LSD-induced fantasy in particular, may become preferable to activities in the outside world. It is more exciting, easier, and seemingly safer to explore the fantastic world within than to bother with the drab and difficult one without. This is what makes it possible for some heavy LSD users to spend months in a one-room apartment, going out only to buy and sell drugs, to get food, and occasionally to visit a friend. To me, with a less well developed fantasy world, their life appeared dull. There seemed to be a sense of constant waiting, waiting for some non-existent action (or, to quote the Beatles, "waiting for the band") to come. Without a drug to pass the time, the boredom might become unbearable.

Not all of the acid-heads I have known have retreated into the woodwork in this manner. In general, though, those who lived more active lives were youths who used many different drugs, to whom LSD was more incidental than central, part of the "street" life-style as a whole, rather than a cult in itself. It is mainly among the more passive users, those for whom LSD use alone has become a master trait, that I have seen extreme aftereffects and great dependence on fantasy.

The shift from reality to fantasy increases the appeal of mysticism and the occult. Acid-heads can become very dogmatic about their occult beliefs; they may concoct elaborate and well-defined theories which they expound to all who will listen, but they have no use for skeptics. I can remember several very intelligent acid-heads who were convinced that people could vanish into thin air if they meditated hard enough, another who was certain that, by willpower, he had reversed the progress of his receding hairline, and two more who believed that they could will passers-by to move in various directions.

Both during and after hallucinogen use, such feelings of enhanced powers or of invulnerability are common. For example, when an LSD user jumps out a window (an exceedingly rare occurrence, but a favorite topic in the newspapers), it is more likely that he thinks that he can fly than that he is trying to commit suicide. I can remember a boy in a New York apartment injecting himself with DMT and saying to me, "We wouldn't be using this needle if we were afraid of hepatitis." Of the three people from that apartment that I followed up later, all got hepatitis from that needle.

Related to this is a feeling of fatalism. Many acid heads believe, in the Eastern manner, that the events of the future are at least partly predetermined. The best way to live is to sit back and let things happen, or as said in the Tao Te Ching, "moving with the stream." For instance, a boy I knew in New York once said:

"I think I'll go to L.A. soon."

"How? You don't have any money."

"Oh, it will happen. I'll be there, I know."

Another example, close to Hinduism, is from a conversation between two heads in Boston: "If you're a homosexual, then that's your karma, that's how you're going to be in this life. Don't try to change it."

The superior satisfaction of fantasy may also cause a decline in sexual activity. The amount of sexual activity among heavy LSD users is remarkably low in light of its apparent availability. An example of this is a conversation between a psychiatrist and a girl who lived with a heavy user.

"You sleep in the same bed with him every night?"

"Yes."

"How often do you have intercourse?"

"Oh, less than once a week."

"Why not more often?"

"Well, he just doesn't seem interested."

Since there is no reason to believe that LSD physiologically affects sexual functions (and assuming, of course, that her boyfriend was not using opiates), the retreat into fantasy seems the best explanation of this.

As fantasy becomes more important, the heavy hallucinogen user draws farther away from the outside world, which has little use for his mystic and occult beliefs, his elaborate theories, and his strange behavior. The greater the importance of the world within, the more he will want to use hallucinogens that in turn further intensify his dependence on fantasy. A similar vicious circle surrounds interpersonal relationships of all kinds. Not only may LSD-fantasy become a substitute for interpersonal relationships, but sharing the drug, as already discussed, becomes the prime mechanism for establishing rapport. The more one depends on the drug for this purpose, the more it is used, and so forth.

Another frequent aftereffect of heavy hallucinogen use is difficulty in coping with aggression, or even in distinguishing it from mere jest. A dramatic example of this (although, strictly speaking, this case represents an effect rather than an aftereffect) occurred in a friend of mine named Terry who had taken STP. He was in a room with friends, one of whom decided to creep up behind him and hit him gently on the head in order to create visual effects in front of his eyes. Terry noticed the boy standing behind him and wondered what was happening. When he turned back and saw that the others were smiling at him, he appeared ill at ease. The friend hit him on the head and everyone laughed good-naturedly, but I sensed that he did not understand that it had been merely a playful gesture. About ten minutes later, when I was talking with him outside, he appeared tremendously anxious and uncomfortable:

"What's wrong?" I asked.

"I feel pains in all my joints, and I feel cold, very cold. It's awful."

On a hunch, I explained to him the incident in the room,

describing each person's emotions, making it clear that the whole thing had been in fun with no aggression implied. He began to understand, and suddenly exclaimed:

"Hey, the pain and the cold — it's gone!"

It has been my fastest therapeutic success to date, a capsule neurosis as it were. Although it occurred in a person actually under the influence of a hallucinogen, it would not be surprising in a heavy user two weeks after his last trip.

Another example is an incident that has occurred several times: A boy asked me a question in a voice so low that I could not possibly hear him. I asked, "What?" He seemed to misinterpret my questioning "what?" as an aggressive "what!" for he huddled in a corner and put his arms over his face. I tried to get him to repeat what he had said, but he thought that I was trying to get him into an argument and would not go on.

This is an extreme case, but typical of users who have centered their lives around LSD. They find it difficult to carry on an argument. If I challenged them for more than a sentence or two, they would say "don't hassle me, man" and switch to another subject. Indeed this phrase is one of the most common ones among heavy LSD users. Deeply involved acid-heads often have a meek, almost fragile quality; one senses that even the slightest aggression might shatter them. It seems better to simply agree with what they say. Some of them even find it something of an ordeal to handle a taxi driver or a man behind a lunch counter. For people with such a low tolerance for interpersonal "hassles," it becomes mandatory to live in a subculture based on "love" and mildness, that is, to stay in the apartment among friends and use more hallucinogens.

I have never quite understood what was meant by the term "psychologically addictive," but if anything, this is it. Just as heroin grips its users in physiological addiction, so the vicious circles of the aftereffects of LSD make the subculture a one-way street with few exits. Many acid-heads are well aware of the dangers of drug use, of disease, and of the law. They dislike the dirt, the smell, the cold and cramped apartments; they feel the boredom of the present, and sense the emptiness of the future. But it is more inviting to take another trip with the others than to try to buck the tide.

X. THE STIMULANTS

The Effects

Stimulants of the central nervous system, particularly amphetamine (Benzedrine, Dexedrine) and methamphetamine (Methedrine, Desoxyn), have risen rapidly in popularity in the last few years. Many reasons for this rise have been discussed in previous chapters under the heading of drug use in general. But there are some effects unique to "speed" that have made it singularly popular today.

Once again, the first and most important reason is that speed is fun. Unlike marijuana or LSD, euphoria is one of its specific, predictable effects. In forty seconds, a shot of fifty milligrams of Methedrine will turn absolute melancholia into giddy happiness and maintain it for several hours; of all common drugs, only cocaine, which is short-lived in its effects and absurdly expensive, exceeds the amphetamines in this respect. Youths who are subject to frequent episodes of depression (in my experience this group included a larger population of girls than of boys) quickly fall in love with amphetamines. Unless one takes too much, speed is practically guaranteed to make one feel happy, at least for awhile. One girl, whom I have known for a long time, described it this way:

> "I get those times when I just feel terrible, and the whole world seems like a photograph in hazy black and white, and I feel shitty, and that I'm never going to do anything, and nothing's ever going to happen. And I look out at the future and it's an endless progression of cloudy days and slow drizzle on the dirty streets, with the orange rinds and the coffee grounds and the garbage floating in the river. And you get the feeling that nothing's ever going to happen, and you go to sleep, but you sleep for about three hours and wake up at four in the morning. It's the sort of time that you might want to smoke grass, so you could fall asleep again, but that's dull. And acid's out of the question; it would be a guaranteed bummer at that time. Right then — that's the time to do speed. You get out your works and shoot up a little bit of it, and suddenly everything is nice to look at again. And for a few hours you feel alive and beautiful and you go out and talk to people and do things."

> "What about alcohol?"

> "You mean taking it when you're depressed? Oh, God, no. That would only make it worse. Then you'd really feel rotten. Alcohol makes you feel sick. Speed makes you *alive!*"

Another girl simply said:

> Amphetamine keeps me from committing suicide.

I have also known many girls like the following one, who took amphetamine for physiologic or psychologic depression near the time of menstruation:

> In my dorm at college, there were quite a few girls who had prescriptions for pills for cramps, and some of the pills contained Dexedrine. So lots of other girls went to the doctor to get prescriptions, and pretended that they had cramps, just so they could get the Dexedrine to keep them from feeling

depressed when they were getting their periods. And then there were a good deal of black-market Dexies and Bennies floating around the dorm for the same reason. Also, the girls got to know the names of doctors who would prescribe them amphetamines to lose weight with. Sometimes they were not particularly interested in losing weight, and they kept the pills around to stay up late at night studying, or for when they felt depressed, or to sell to friends.

This is one reason why so many girls become heavy amphetamine users: they have a much greater opportunity to be introduced to it through prescription diet pills or pills for cramps, or they obtain pills from other girls who do have prescriptions.

A second major attraction of amphetamine is its ability to make one confident, outgoing, and talkative. This effect is more frequently sought by boys. As one described it:

Speed is a great thing if you feel a little shy about talking to people. After you've taken two or three dexies, you suddenly lose all your inhibitions about walking up and making conversation with somebody. Like you're going to a dance and want to meet some girls, or it's a summer evening and all the street people have gathered in the park, and you want to be able to just start rapping with some new people. It's just a great thing that way — it makes it so you can walk up to a group of people and join in with them. Of course if you take too much, you get so talkative that you scare people away, except of course if other people are also speeding. But if you take the right amount, it's a great thing.

When two people are both on amphetamine, they may exchange more words in four hours of converstation than in days of normal existence:

When you really want to get into a heavy rap with somebody, speed is absolutely the greatest thing going. You feel much less inhibited about talking about things that really matter to you and you feel more trusting of somebody that you're talking to — I mean it makes you just instinctively want to socialize more. It's really wonderful when you're meeting somebody for the first time – you take speed together, and you find out everything about each other in six hours of constant rapping. It makes it as if you'd known each other for a couple of months. And then it's also nice if you want a rap with somebody you already know well – you can find out new things about each other that you never knew before. It's a great thing!

A third attribute of amphetamines is that they must be injected for maximum effect. Most hallucinogens (with the exception of DMT and its relatives) do not produce any immediate effects when injected, because they diffuse too slowly across the blood-brain barrier. But in individuals who have not developed too much tolerance, amphetamines produce an extraordinary "rush" that begins within seconds and grows more intense for two or three minutes, a sensation of utter euphoria, seemingly centered right in the brain, coupled with a pleasant tingling throughout the body. A boy in New York attempted to describe it:

I hadn't gotten off on the DMT the previous night, and then when we did cocaine everybody again got off but nothing happened to me at all. So when the time came to do speed, they said, "We'll really fix this guy!" So they poured this absolute mountain of meth into a spoon and shot it into me. For about fifteen seconds nothing happened, and then suddenly it felt like someone was turning on banks of photoflash bulbs in my brain, first a few, and then hundreds and then thousands. I just fell down on the floor and rolled around in ecstacy. The pleasure was so great that it was all I could do just to absorb it all. My whole body was just switched on with an electric aliveness. And for the next eight hours, man, I was on top of the world!

But the importance of the needle goes far beyond the effects themselves. The psychoanalyst would suggest that this may be due to the sexual symbolism of being entered by the needle and receiving an orgasm-like rush from the drug. Phallic imagery aside, no sexual interaction with another human being is so reliable or so certain to cure depression. Whatever its other implications, the needle is a measure of one's experience in the subculture, particularly if one has learned to perform the injection alone. Often there is a definite series of steps taught to each initiate so that he can learn to "hit himself." First, he must learn to watch the injection instead of looking away. Then he performs the subsidiary act of holding the tie-cord around his upper arm, and finally, he learns to perform the entire operation by himself with increasing competence and speed.

No matter how expert one becomes at performing the injection, it is still a painful and risky process, the mark of a deep commitment to the drug world. Even many experienced users still shun injections. "Man, I'm into drugs, but works are a bad scene!" they will say. Those who do become accustomed to the needle constitute a special group, both pitied and admired by others. Among these individuals, the ritual of injection constantly reaffirms the unity of the group and the commitment of its members.

But even with these attractions, amphetamines could not have become so important without the prior existence of a subculture founded on marijuana and the hallucinogens. A few youths — particularly girls who have been introduced to amphetamine through diet pills — may become heavy amphetamine users without even flirting with the hallucinogens, but the vast majority spend some period using many different drugs before they reach the point of injecting amphetamine on a regular basis. The initial period allows them to learn the essentials in the subculture: how to cope with the illegality and dangers of the drugs, how to relate to other users, how to deal, how to perform injections, and hundreds of smaller details. Once they have tried speed and lost their fears of shooting it, they may combine it with hallucinogen use, or they may abandon hallucinogens almost entirely, becoming exclusive amphetamine users: "speed freaks." The following account is from a speed freak who had been shooting methamphetamine for about ten months:

> I used to do a lot of acid, a lot of grass, sometimes mescaline — you know, lots of stuff. But acid got to be sort of a drag. It got so that I just didn't like it anymore. I just didn't like to have my mind screwed up like that. You know — it just wasn't fun, it was too heavy, man. I guess the reason I got turned on to Methedrine was that it made my mind all clear

instead of paranoid like it was on acid, and on grass, too. But with speed you never get paranoid. Well, maybe some people do, and of course you do sometimes when you're crashing, but when you've shot it up you feel so nice and everything just fits into place and you feel really alive and everything. Anyhow, I never do acid or other stuff anymore. Sometimes I do grass to fall asleep when I crash, but more often I do some other down — a barb or Thorazine, or heroin. Heroin is really good for falling asleep when you're crashing, but it's more expensive.

A girl, Tania, had been injecting amphetamine and cocaine for nearly three years when I met her in 1969. She had reached a level of nearly two grams of amphetamine per day:

"Oh, man, it's the only thing, the only thing to do. Without speed, drugs wouldn't be worth it. It's so much more pleasant than acid. You get used to it, you know? It's nice. You get accustomed to it."

"How come you stopped doing acid and grass in favor of ups?"

"Because they feel good. Acid is too heavy. It doesn't always feel good, you know? I love it — I'm just not interested in doing other things. Speed is just what I'm into. I don't know. I just think it's a — I don't know — it's a nice thing."

Since I never took notes in the presence of users, I have only approximated Tania's exact words, but they give some idea of her confused state. Three months ago she died, or so I was told by one of her neighbors. Nobody informed her parents, who live somewhere in western New York. Nobody even knew her last name.

Disillusionment with LSD and its relatives — too may bad trips, too much anxiety, failure to cope with depression — is the most frequent reason that I have heard for the exclusive use of amphetamines. Superimposed upon this, particularly among people like Tania who began shooting high doses at regular intervals, is psychic and possibly physical habituation to the drug: amphetamine becomes the center of life, and one has neither time nor inclination to return to hallucinogens.

Cocaine is roughly similar to amphetamine in its effects, although a potent analgesic as well. But it is unimportant, for it is so expensive that few youths can afford to use it on a regular basis. Since the effects last only about fifteen minutes, one has to shoot it over and over to keep going, and two or three people could possibly go through hundreds of dollars worth of cocaine in an evening. Among those who do use cocaine, the reasons are much the same as for amphetamines: for euphoria (particularly the rush after the injection) to abolish depression, to produce self-confidence and aggressiveness, or out of curiosity, as an adjunct to other drug use.

The Aftereffects

As with the hallucinogens, the aftereffects of the amphetamines help to further perpetuate use and to reinforce the unity of the subculture. Probably the best known of these is the crash after a dose has worn off, comparable to the hangover from alcohol in that it is a short-term reaction which can be relieved by another dose. But unlike the hangover, the crash is more mental than physical: its primary feature is intense depression. A boy who had experienced many crashes described them as follows:

> If you've been speeding for forty-eight or seventy-two hours, then the crash gets really bad. You know that your depression is just caused by coming off the drug, and you keep repeating that to yourself, but it just doesn't help. It's absolutely impossible to philosophize or psychologize your way out of it. More than once I have sat in a room contemplating the fifth-story window and debating whether or not it was worth the effort to go over and jump out of it. You never do jump out, of course, but it feels like you're on the verge of it. I really hate the feeling. You really have to pay the price for all the fun you had when you were speeding. The best thing of course is to have a down handy, like a barbiturate so you can fall asleep. But if you don't have any downs, you absolutely can't sleep. You just sit there in limbo between sleep and wakefulness.

Paranoia is frequent during the crash, and some users experience hallucinations or even some degree of catatonia. Since another dose will postpone the crash for a few more hours, there is a great temptation to take more and more amphetamine. Thus, a four-day amphetamine jag is not uncommon, and some users stay awake, eating practically nothing, for a week. By the end of this period they may be totally confused and constantly hallucinating, but to some a continuation of this is preferable to an immediate crash. The crash is important in that it places the user in a vulnerable and suggestable position in which he is dependent on his friends. Once he has gone through this ordeal with a group of people, he often feels closer to them: the experience of common suffering, as in battles or concentration camps, helps to unite the group.

Unlike "LSD psychosis", the crash after several days of continuous heavy amphetamine use is often practically indistinguishable from classical schizophrenic symptoms: catatonia, inappropriate affect, visual and auditory hallucinations, and, most often, severe paranoia. On two occasions I have spent more than an hour trying to persuade a crashing amphetamine user to take a dose of Thorazine, only to have him repeatedly accuse me of plotting against him and trying to make him feel worse. Such psychoses, when they occur, produce the same consequences as the aftereffects of LSD: impaired reality testing and decreased ability to cope with the interactions and aggressions of the outside world. The paranoia seems particularly important, because it is often directed at the police, government officials, and other figures in the outside world, with consequent reassertion of the subcultural identity.

Although heavy users do not experience marked physical withdrawal symptoms from amphetamine, tolerance and craving develop rapidly. Although a shot of 2 mg. of methamphetamine will produce noticeable effects in an ordinary individual, and 250 mg will probably kill him, I have known many speed freaks who injected more than a gram per day. Depending on sources of supply, this may cost from $30 to $200 a week, which most of them earn by dealing. Despite the relative lack of physical withdrawal symptoms, the craving for another dose is overwhelming – enough to eclipse the need for any psychological support from the subculture. Unlike hallucinogens, amphetamine can perpetuate itself indefinitely even in a lone user.

Amphetamine dependence, as I have seen it, is more pathetic than addiction to opiates. Morphine at least, produces practically no direct physical damage to the body, even after years of use, although most addicts suffer from subsidiary problems. But speed freaks are emaciated because they cannot feel hunger, chalk-white from lack of hemoglobin, afflicted with lapses of memory and attention, sometimes psychotic. It is universally believed in the drug world that amphetamine kills brain cells and that three years of heavy use will reduce the brain to the consistency of peanut butter — the smooth-spreading brand. I have heard gruesome stories about deceased amphetamine addicts whose brains, when removed for examination at autopsy, crumbled to pieces in the hands of the pathologist. This is not clearly substantiated in the medical literature, but many speed freaks have told me that they noticed fogginess in their thought and serious lapses of memory between the fourth and fifteenth month of constant use. In some, these symptoms merely drove them to more amphetamine, because it was the only way in which they could seemingly rejuvenate, albeit transiently, their mental powers. The most dilapidated users resembled people with Korsakoff's psychosis, a disease usually caused by alcoholism. Their retention span was reduced to seconds, and their conversation was a continuous stream of *non sequiturs* and fanciful memories. Living in this morbid state, speed freaks usually remain, to the end, in the arms of the subculture, for only the street people, with their wonderful tolerance for all manner of unfortunate or rejected individuals, will accept them.

XI THE DEPRESSANTS

Things are Different Today

Probably the most malignant feature of drug use in the 1970's is the popularity of a diverse group of drugs most conveniently grouped as "depressants": tranquilizers, alcohol, barbiturates, and heroin and other opiates. Only two or three years ago, few youths became deeply involved with "downs;" they wanted to be turned on rather than turned off. But now, many communities have become like the one described by this 17-year-old boy in New Jersey:

> "A year ago, everybody in my town was doing a lot of tripping and speeding, and only doing downs once in awhile. You know, things to get to sleep when you're crashing or to get down from a bad trip — things like that. We used to do alcohol sometimes, but not much. Now all of the real heads have shifted over to downs, especially to skag. The only thing anybody wants to get into around here any more is a good nod."

"Why did everybody get into downs?"

"I don't know. Everybody just got so that they weren't turned on to tripping anymore. They just decided that downs were the best kind of experience to have."

Why are opiates so attractive? To begin with, they are fun, but a different fun from the colorful and fast-moving world of the hallucinogens and stimulants: a relaxation of body and mind, loss of anxiety, flattening of the emotions, and gentle, subtle euphoria. Many youths are unimpressed by their first opiate experiences; they have to learn to like the effects:

> The first time I smoked opium I couldn't understand why everybody thought it was so cool. It just sort of annihilated me. I just sat there with my mouth hanging open and my face sagging, staring at the wall. I stared at the wall for like half an hour before I decided that it might be interesting to contemplate the ceiling. So I contemplated the ceiling for half an hour. I remember thinking to myself that this was a bore, and how did people ever get addicted to skag and so forth.

> But then after I'd done it two or three times I began to appreciate it. It's like good wine — you have to educate yourself to really enjoy it. I began to realize that there was something really nice about opium, to just sit there with every ounce of tension gone from your body, and nod and dream pleasant dreams. It's really nice for your imagination. You can turn on almost any image you want, and sit and contemplate it for awhile, and then turn on a different one.

A college student named Lew, who injected heroin and other opiates about three times a week, described the effects with even more enthusiasm:

> The dreams you get are really hallucinations. They're so vivid that you think you are really living them. A weekend of shooting heroin is to me like an orgy — a state of complete satiation of all of your tensions and desires. You can sit there and live in whatever world you please, far from all of the cold and pain of the

real world. Heroin is the king of drugs. After you've become used to it, the idea of going back to acid or speed is just absurd. They just don't satisfy like heroin.

It's a nuisance that heroin is so damn addictive. I have to be very careful about how I use it. After spending three orgiastic days down in New York over the weekend, I come back up here and force myself not to take any for several days. Sometimes I take a little alcohol if I have too strong a craving for more heroin. So I've been able to manage it pretty well.

One of the nicest things about heroin is the day after. You sleep like a baby the night after you've shot up, and when you wake up the next day, you feel beautifully refreshed and still relaxed because there's a little left in your system. I can remember just yesterday as I was talking to my thesis advisor in his office, I felt so at ease and comfortable but still alert. The day after is practically the best thing about it.

Lew may initially have tried heroin merely out of curiosity, to complete his list of drug experiences, because it was "tough," or because he was trying to deal with loneliness or sexual frustration. But heroin quickly became a necessary part of his life: an outlet for sexual energy, an amplifier of fantasy, and a relief from the anxiety which he experienced in college. Ultimately, he found permanent relief in suicide.

Anxiety may lead to opiate, barbiturate, or alcohol use in the manner that depression leads to amphetamines. Anxiety seems to be particularly frequent among those who have used other drugs for two or three years, for reasons that are difficult to specify. A girl in Boston attempted to explain this:

It's been four years now since the first time I smoked grass. I began in the first year thinking that grass was really nice, and I did it a lot. Then I got interested in other drugs, and I spent the next year getting introduced to acid and mescaline and STP and so on, and also to speed. Then in the third year I got into it really heavily and tripped once a week maybe and took grass a lot. And then towards the end of the third year, I began to not like tripping anymore. It got so that I would get frightened easily, and I'd get upset about having my mind out of control. It got so that I would be almost sure I was going to have a bad trip before I even swallowed the cap, and of course I started having bummers just because I was expecting them. Even grass got so that it was not as pleasant. When everybody else wanted to get stoned, I'd feel sort of reluctant. I'd be afraid that I was going to get paranoid, or that it would simply be a bore. And speed got to be sort of a bad scene, too. I found that if I took too much I'd get sort of scared on that, too. So that's when I began to use downs more. I began to think that opium and barbiturates and heroin and so on were pretty good after all. Because they're predictable — they are certain not to get you into a heavy anxiety thing. They take you away from anxiety rather than toward it. So now in the fourth year I have been doing mostly Seconal and Darvon and heroin and stuff like that.

A boy from Maryland named Greg experienced the same progression:

I first got stoned when I was 15, and it was cool. Everybody did it all the time, and we always had a great time. And then we got into acid and MDA and other stuff and that was really beautiful and exciting, and we always had good trips. We did speed once in a while and smoked opium when we could get it, and the ones who had the balls to do it shot up skag. And then a funny thing happened to me that seemed to happen to some of the other guys, too. We got to feeling that tripping was too heavy, that it just wasn't the pleasant thing it used to be. It just wasn't fun anymore. Most of us kept tripping because we wanted to go along with the rest, and of course, there were other kids coming in all the time, just getting started doing acid, and we would trip with them because they were so enthusiastic about it. But after about another year I just didn't like tripping anymore. It just wasn't enjoyable, you know? It was a hassle. And so what a lot of my friends and I did was to get into heroin. Because that way you didn't lose your cool — you were still taking big drugs and everybody still considered you to be OK — but you didn't have to get into bad trips and paranoid things anymore.

The ones of us who had gotten into downs considered ourselves to be sort of the old timers, the ones who had done all the experimenting around and had settled down to the good old downs. So when somebody else was doing acid, I'd do a couple of Dilaudids or four Talwins and go off into my own thing. Also a lot of us have sort of come full circle to alcohol. After you've been blowing your mind with all sorts of other stuff, booze is a pretty good thing. You get so that you understand why it's been so popular for the last five thousand years.

Another opiate user, named Bert, going to college in western Massachusetts, had similar thoughts about his "youth" in the drug world:

Looking back three years, it's hard to believe that I was really so freaky, eating acid like it was going out of style. If you gave me a cap of acid now, I'd have a bummer. I guess I'm getting old. I'm not so wild and free, and for me skag is the only drug now.

These accounts are typical of dozens that I have heard: a sequence beginning with marijuana, then a rise to a plateau of hallucinogen use, followed by anxiety, disenchantment with hallucinogens, and a retreat to opiates, barbiturates, and alcohol. Like Bert, many are almost frightened when they reminisce about their earlier years; they cannot believe that they used to be so bold. Perhaps this is because they have experienced or witnessed bad hallucinogenic aftereffects, or perhaps they have felt uncomfortably close to the law. For many, it may simply be a consequence of growing up: they became less interested in experimenting, more attuned to stability, relaxation, and avoidance of anxiety. Whatever the origins of the process, it seems to affect the majority of users. A few, to be sure, continue using hallucinogens year after year without seeiming to lose their enthusiasm, but most either drop out of drug use entirely or turn to the depressants.

Most often, then, depressant use follows an initial period of membership in the general adolescent drug subculture. Though the subculture may be primarily concerned with hallucinogens or amphetamines, it still presents many opportunities to try depressants of all kinds. Thorazine is the most popular antidote for bad trips, but many users try Librium, Valium, Miltown, Seconal, Nembutal, and other sedatives as well. Amphetamine users keep a supply of barbiturates or opiates handy for falling asleep during the crash. Depressants are also common as an adjunct to other drugs: marijuana is often smoked with opium, amphetamine taken with a barbiturate to enhance the euphoria, or cocaine shot in one arm and heroin in the other. With so many opportunities to try depressants incidentally in the course of other drug use, a youth may find that he prefers them in their own right. Thus, even though he has little interest in depressants *per se* a youth is almost sure to try them.

But long before he has even heard of the drug culture, a youth is introduced to depressants by his parents and American culture as a whole. Even young children in the most rural parts of the country have witnessed an adult severely intoxicated with alcohol, and they often find that their parents are more tolerant of this than of even the mildest marijuana use. Perhaps, as a result, depressant use inspires less guilt or anxiety in youths than does marijuana or the hallucinogens. Since it conflicts less with childhood learning experiences, heroin may actually seem more comfortable and natural than LSD. Perhaps this is why Greg "came full circle" to alcohol, or Bert abandoned hallucinogens for heroin — both were expressing, in a peculiar way, what they had been taught as children.

Not only do parents set an example through alcohol, but a great many of them use other depressants as well: the 1,000,000 pounds of barbiturates consumed in this country every year have been supplemented with all manner of other sedatives and "tranquilizers": Noludar, Miltown, Librium, Valium, Sinequan, Thorazine, Compazine, Mellaril, and scores of others. On more than one occasion, glancing into a medicine chest in an ordinary home, I have identified five or six different sedatives and tranquilizers, not to mention codeine, Darvon, Talwin, Demerol, and other potent pain-killers.

Most youths are very conscious of the drug use of the older generation. It has even become a subject for rock songs, such as "Mother's Little Helper" on the Rolling Stones' album, "Flowers":

Things are different today.
I hear every mother say,
"Mother needs something today to calm her down."
And though she's not really ill,
There's a little yellow pill.
She goes running for the shelter
Of her "mother's little helper."
And it helps her on her way,
Gets her through her busy day.

It is difficult to assess the effect of such parents on a child, but if, when he is older, they attack him for smoking marijuana or taking LSD, he might aptly remind them that the older generation gets the younger generation it deserves.

Addiction

Whether they are introduced to depressants by their parents or their peers, most youths continue to use them for pleasure, to deal with anxiety, or, as in Greg's case, to maintain rapport with their friends after ceasing to use hallucinogens or stimulants. Depressant use is further perpetuated by many of the mechanisms already discussed for the general case of drug subcultures. In particular, heroin use, like amphetamine use, is encouraged by the cult of the needle and the pleasure of the rush. It may function as a continuing demonstration of toughness, or even as a sort of identity, an adequate thing to be doing with one's life. But unlike the hallucinogens and stimulants, the depressants have a special weapon of their own: practically all produce frank physical dependence. Addiction to alcohol or heroin compares only with amphetamine dependence as the most unhappy sight that I have seen in the drug world.

Contrary to popular belief, one does not automatically become a heroin addict after one or two doses; many days of continuous heavy use are required before any signs of physical dependence appear. I have talked to two boys who used heroin every day for a week without noticing physical withdrawal symptoms afterwards. I have known others who used heroin fifty or one hundred times in the course of two years, without ever experiencing a craving for another dose. Of course there are youths at the opposite end of the spectrum; I met one who had become addicted over the course of six months of rapidly increasing use. But his story is exceptional; of the youths I have known who had tried heroin, the great majority were not addicted.

Another common misconception is that heroin, like the Sirens, is impossible to renounce after one has first tasted its delights, that it seduces its victims into addiction. Admittedly, heroin is usually enjoyable, particularly if one is suffering from a great deal of anxiety or any sort of physical pain. But the actual pleasure of heroin was not overly important in the accounts of users I have known; in fact most could remember very unpleasant experiences, especially when they had taken too much. In particular many recalled their first dose as a miserable combination of nausea, malaise, and fear. The following description from a high school student is typical of several that I have heard:

> "I got really scared when I began to feel that feeling of relaxation spreading through me. I felt sort of like my whole body was falling apart, like I was turning into a big blob of jelly or something. I wanted it to go away, but it came on more and more. After a few minutes it got so that I wanted to fall asleep, but just as I began to doze off, I got this fear that I might never wake up again, like I was going to die. And also I got really sick to my stomach. I didn't actually blow lunch, but I felt like I was about to for about three hours."

> "Why did you shoot skag again after having such a bad experience the first time?"

> "Well, I don't know. I guess I figured that it would be better the next time. Like other people could get a good high out of it, so I figured I ought to be able to, too. And I did. Like now I never get scared and it's real nice."

> "Do you think you would have taken it again if there weren't any other people around who were taking it?"

> "Well, I wouldn't have known how to get more of it if I hadn't had friends who knew where to get good

stuff. Like it's a really bad scene to go down and try to score with some cat you've never seen on a street corner. It's a bad scene — you're almost guaranteed to get burned in a scene like that."

"But suppose you were able to get good stuff. Would you have taken it again if you were all alone, do you think?"

"I don't know. Maybe I wouldn't have. It's sort of hard to imagine what that would be like because there's always been lots of other kids around who were doing drugs."

For this boy, as for most other users, the subculture was not only necessary for supply, but important as a source of encouragement.

In short, the actual effects of heroin play a secondary role in the process of addiction. For the addicts that I have known, the process was grounded in childhood experiences and in alienation from American society, then was powerfully reinforced by the presence of the drug subculture. Only much later did craving become important. Once physical addiction has set in, however, psychological support from the subculture becomes unnecessary; chemistry alone will ensure continued use. But heroin addicts rarely become loners; they still turn to others for supply and usually for companionship as well. In general they associate with other addicts and therefore move into a subculture of their own, merging with the lower-class heroin subculture and drawing away from the group of drug-using youths that I have described. I have seen relatively little of the addict subculture, because fewer than one in one hundred of the users I have known has reached it. Heroin addiction, fortunately, is still a rare conclusion to a drug career among middle- to upper-class youths, although it may be much more frequent in five or ten years.

Unlike the material in previous chapters, the long-term effects of heroin addiction — malnutrition, disease, and crime — are fairly well known to the public, for the plight of young addicts has recently become a favorite subject in the media. Graphic newspaper articles and television documentaries about addicts have alarmed many Americans. Yet for all of their alarm, many parents may prefer to hear about this most extreme little fraction of drug users, for unlike marijuana or LSD, heroin seems comfortably remote from home. It is a pleasant illusion that the faceless victim of an overdose, just described in a national newscast, could not really have come from a nice family in a nice community like one's own.

The first section of this book ended with a description of a few of the "good" conclusions to a drug career: interest in Eastern philosophy, communal living, or a return to school to study some field of genuine interest. This section has described the dangerous conclusions. What is the ratio between the two? What is the incidence of "casualties" among users?

Even allowing that one could define "casualties," it would be necessary to talk to the same group of users ten years from now; the phenomenon of widespread drug use among middle- to upper-class youths is too recent to permit an assessment of its ultimate dangers and benefits. Nevertheless, I am certain that the dangers are far less than is popularly supposed. I believe that more than 95% of the users I have known have incurred no more permanent physical or psychological harm from drug use than from the socially approved forms of adolescent experimentation. And many have almost surely learned more — about themselves, about relating to others, about their society, about the paths to fulfillment — than they would have if they had never been exposed to drug use or the drug subculture.

The last 5% include some great tragedies, particularly among those who become dependent on amphetamine or addicted to heroin. I have not tried to minimize this during the last two chapters, but the reader must bear in mind that they represent a small minority of users. It is odd that so many people equate all drug use with its evil extremes; Americans have always seemed capable of ignoring the comparable fraction of social drinkers whose lives are ultimately ruined by alcohol addiction. But then, alcohol is ancient and familiar, whereas the drug scene is, to most adults, new and frightening.

XII. THE PROBLEM

Everyone talks of the "drug problem," yet we are only beginning to understand where the real problems lie. First, drug use is a response to the syndrome of alienation from American society. Drug use ranges from simple fun — a transient relief from boredom — to an entire way of life, an identity which buffers against apathy. Hallucinogens, in particular, can become a means for a psychological or philosophical quest, a search for meaning in a society perceived as unloving, lonely, and meaningless. To criticize exclusively the personality of a user, as some do, is to ignore the faults of the culture to which he is reacting.

Since alienation will not soon vanish from America, it will remain a foundation of drug use for years to come. But for the present, many youths have found alternate ways to deal with it, among them Eastern philosophies and religions, communal life, attempts at social, political, and environmental reform, and personally meaningful intellectual pursuit. Though drug use may lose little of its appeal during the next years, these alternatives are gaining in popularity, and will continue to do so.

Second, drug use and the subculture as a whole are reactions to the isolation of home. Drugs may represent a release from shelter, a test of competence, an expression of anger, and very often, a step away from loneliness. Many parents, acting with genuine love and an attempt at understanding, are unintentionally encouraging drug use in their children by denying them other ways to grow up.

Family life, like the rest of our society, will not change rapidly; many more youths will feel too sheltered and too lonely. Women's liberation, I feel, is a hope for the future: it may lead to a new generation of mothers not so desperately bound to their children, and fathers not so remote. But the more immediate answer is knowledge: parents must learn to appreciate how powerful the feelings of shelter or loneliness can be, and how imperative it is for their children to express them.

Third, drugs are surrounded by a complex subculture, the attractions of which are superimposed upon, and colored by, the effects and long-term aftereffects of use. The particular drugs chosen by a youth, the frequency with which he uses them, and the group with which he associates — all these determine whether his experiences will be enlightening or destructive, benign or catastrophic. Once again, the problem is usually lack of knowledge. Many intelligent adults, despite serious concern, have not learned to distinguish between vastly different forms of drug use. They exaggerate the evils of some drugs and deny those of others: a marijuana cigarette constitutes "drug abuse," three martinis do not. However innocent their ignorance they forfeit the respect of their children in this way. Those who extend their criticisms of drug use to the point of great anger, whatever their reasons, may only stimulate what they are striving to suppress.

In this area, above all others, knowledge is essential. In criticizing ignorance, I have perhaps been unduly hard on the older generation. In part this reflects a loyalty to my own, and sympathy with the users who are my friends. More importantly, it attempts to counterbalance those voices which heap excessive blame on the users alone, or the chemicals they use, while denying the deeper problems. I hope that my descriptions of many real human beings, the presentation of their thoughts and feelings, and the glimpses into their individuality, might stimulate better communication between users and their critics and lead ultimately to deeper and warmer understanding.

APPENDIX

The Methods Used in This Study

The more scientifically inclined reader has doubtless raised many questions about the techniques used in this study. Have I known a random sample of drug users? Was I ever "put on?" To what degree have my own beliefs biased my data? Is it even possible to do a study like this and emerge with valid generalizations? The following is an answer to these questions.

I became interested in the hippies, as they were then known, in the spring of 1967. The interest was not academic; like many of my college friends, I harbored fantasies of joining their world, or rather, what I imagined to be their world at the time. In the summer of 1967 I visited Haight-Ashbury in San Francisco. It took awhile to find any hippies among the crowds of tourists, but I saw enough to discover that life for most of them was different from what I had imagined, and even more remote from the ideas of the general public.

Returning to college that fall, I had become so interested in drug use that I decided to study it with my tutor, Erik Erikson. His first suggestion was, "Skip, don't have in mind specific questions to which you intend to get an answer. Just go out and live there for awhile; look around you and see what feelings come to you, and I think you will find many things to write about." It was good advice. Had I assumed a more formal attitude towards my study, I might always have remained on the periphery, an observer rather than a participant-observer, missing much of the emotional core of the drug subculture.

That fall, I began to frequent the north side of Beacon Hill in Boston, where I spent many days and nights with several groups of heavy users. Though at first an outsider, I rapidly came to feel at home with them. Most of those I met have since vanished, but a few became friends whom I have seen ever since.

In midwinter, in the beginning of 1968, I made my first visit to the Lower East Side in New York. The scene there was similar to Boston, but "heavier;" youths there were more deeply involved with amphetamines and heroin, more remote from the rest of the world, and destined, it seemed, to remain forever in their little apartments. For some of them, time has proved me wrong; two are back in college, one has just gone to India to study yoga, one has joined a thriving commune in California, and one, still taking LSD three times a year, is a businessman on Wall Street! But about half of those I have followed are scattered around the country, still using drugs, although less heavily than before.

The most exciting period for me was the summer of 1968, when I spent practically all of my time in the Boston street scene. It began on a morning in July when I sat down by a tree on Boston Common. Within eight hours, I found myself working with a dozen others on the *Common Newsletter,* which put out its first two-page issue two days later and seven more during the next six weeks. The *Newsletter* kept me at the center of things for nearly two months, working to find articles, searching for a mimeograph machine, collecting nickel contributions for it on the Common, and getting to know many of the thousand-odd youths who read it. I talked with police, narcotics agents, representatives of the Mayor, ministers, doctors, those who wanted to help and those who wanted to throw the whole crowd in jail. I was present at the rock concerts, the political rallies, and most of the police incidents, although unlike most of the rest of the *Newsletter* staff, I managed to stay out of jail.

I left the Common in August. The *Newsletter* survived only a little longer; most of the hippies diffused to other cities, rented apartments on Beacon Hill and elsewhere in Boston, or went back to school. When I returned for my last year of college only a few weeks later, the Common was almost bare. I walked sadly across the grass where I had spent so many days and evenings, seeing only a police car ominously parked at one corner, and a few well-dressed adults who had come to peer at the hippies before it was all over. As in Haight-Ashbury the summer before, the visitors spent most of their time peering at each other.

In college that year, many of my friends came to visit me. Most were from the East Coast, but a few drifted in from as far away as Texas and California. Some had acquired new interests, but many were still using drugs; one, a big dealer, arrived with the police only ten minutes behind! With these friends I exchanged accounts about old times, the latest activities of those we knew, and impressions of the scene and how it was changing. At the same time, I saw a great deal of college drug use, not only at Harvard, but all over the East. Though my experiences in college were less dramatic than in the streets, I learned a great deal from them, particularly from conversations with intellectual users who had attempted to analyze what was going on in their heads and in society. They provided many little gems of insight, some of which I have quoted.

In 1969, with this background, I wrote my college thesis about drug use — an academic, heavily-footnoted work that lacked some of the warmth I had wanted to transmit. In late 1970, I was asked to revise my thesis for a non-technical book. It was easy to bring myself up to date; I visited many old friends and talked with new ones, particularly those who were familiar with areas of drug use most remote from me, such as the high-school scene in the Midwest and West. Though the total group represented more than twenty-five states and ranged in age from twelve to seventy, their accounts fitted together surprisingly well. I found that the magnitude of the scene and its overall flavor had changed greatly, but the fundamental reasons for drug use were much the same. After several months of new experiences and many hours of conversations, I was able to write the revised version with confidence.

Although I have read several hundred books and articles, the best of which are cited in the reference notes, reading contributed little to my understanding of the actual workings of the subculture and the feelings of those within it; the sources for this book were people. There is no other way in which I would have learned what I did: whatever the drawbacks of participant-observation, it is the best method for understanding the social psychology of a deviant subculture.

What are the drawbacks? First, it is impossible to know a "random sample" of users, a concept difficult even to imagine in this case. Since I have known users in dozens of localities around the country, and since I made no attempt to control which ones I met, sampling was probably not a severe source of error. Though I have known more users from the East than the West and more of college age than of high-school age, I have known enough from any given background to be able to extrapolate to their group as a whole. Furthermore, to ensure that I was not losing track of any important group of users, I have constantly tried to check my impressions against those of people familiar with parts of the scene most distant from me. As a final check, I have given my manuscript, at one stage or another, to many readers, ranging from high-school users to physicians. Their feedback helped me to correct a number of wrong impressions.

Finally, the conclusions do not even require a perfect sample, because they do not attempt to be statistically precise; most statements in this book are restricted to adjectives such as "many" and "few." Indeed, even allowing that one could obtain the ideal random sample, an accurate statistical work about drug users could not be written. Many drug users are far too disenchanted with society to respond openly to someone who used such straight techniques as taking notes, distributing questionnaries, or even informal interviewing. Even if the interviewer were under thirty and had long hair, I shudder to think of the result if he asked an acid-head to rate himself on a scale of one to five. A researcher who tried to reduce people to numbers would be fair game for a put-on.

Was I ever put on? That is, did any users deliberately try to deceive me? No doubt this happened occasionally, but it is very unlikely that this would have significantly distorted my overall results. Since most users treated me as a participant rather than an observer, they felt no reason to consciously deceive me. As for their unconscious defenses, I have had to rely on my knowledge of psychology and my past experience with the group as a whole. When I suspected a distortion of facts (as, for example, when Kim said that he had been assaulted in the police van), I compared the account of a second person. Usually it emerged that I had not been put on at all.

A more serious problem is the converse of the above: was I too *close* to the group? How can this book be objective? The answer to this is that of course it is not objective, nor does it pretend to be. Though I have tried to refrain from specific medical or legal opinions, I have not attempted to hide my personal sympathies and criticisms. There are two reasons for this. First, as already discussed, the drug subculture cannot be accurately studied with objective techniques, however desirable they may be. Secondly, as Rosenthal and others have shown, experimenter bias can profoundly influence even those results obtained under the strictest laboratory conditions.* In a participant-observation study, it seems wiser, and more human, for the researcher to reveal his personal feelings, allowing the reader to judge for himself the degree of bias.

The final argument for the validity of the conclusions is simply that they are modest; they do not leap far beyond what I have actually heard and witnessed. At times, the reader may have found this approach disappointing, for the data obtained stands in a cloudy intermediate zone between the imposing precision of the laboratory study and the clinical thoroughness of the individual case history. But participant-observation provides a great deal of information not accessible to either of these techniques: an idea of the inner workings of the subculture and the day-to-day actions and feelings of its members. This information is essential for an understanding of drug use.

*See R. Rosenthal, The social psychology of the psychological experiment. *Amer. Sci.* 1963, 51: 268, for a review of this.

REFERENCE NOTES

Chapter I. The incidence of drug use among various populations of Americans is difficult to study. Even allowing that one can approach the ideal of a random sample, one cannot predict exactly how people will respond when asked if they have done something illegal. Many drug users would refuse even to answer a statistically oriented survey, not because it would be incriminating, but because formal studies would strike them as Establishment-oriented and inhuman. Informal interviewing of users lacks this problem but introduces opposite biases: users often overestimate the incidence of drug use in their schools or communities. Since it is difficult to collect reliable data about this, the estimates in the first chapter have been necessarily guarded and vague.

With these precautions, then, see:

Black, S.; Owens, K. L.; and Wolff, R. P. 1970. Patterns of drug use: A study of 5,482 subjects. *Amer. J. Psychiat.* 127(4): 420-23.

Blum, R. H.; et al. 1970. *Students and drugs.* San Francisco: Jossey-Bass, Inc. A long text with further references.

Mizner, G. L.; Barter, J. T.; and Werme, P. H. 1970. Patterns of drug use among college students: A preliminary report. *Amer. J. Psychiat.* 127: 55-64.

Pope, H.; Walters, P. W.; and Goethals, G. W. Drug use and life style among 500 college undergraduates. In preparation.

Smith, B. C. 1970. Drug use on a university campus. *J. Amer. Coll. Health Assoc.* 18: 360-65.

For some historical interest, see:

Goldstein, R. 1966. *One in seven – drugs on campus.* New York: Walker.

McGlothlin, W. H.; and Cohen, S. 1965. The use of hallucinogenic drugs among college students. *Amer. J. Psychiat.* 122(5): 572-74.

Chapter II. I once asked Lauren what books he had liked. He thought of three, all of which give a glimpse of his philosophy of life:

Fromm, E. 1956. *The art of loving.* New York: Harper and Row.

Heinlein, R. A. 1961. *Stranger in a strange land.* New York: Berkeley Medallion Books.

Huxley, A. 1962. *Island.* New York: Harper and Row.

Chapter III. For some interesting commentary on American high schools, see:

Friedenberg, E. Z. 1963. *Coming of age in America.* New York: Random House, Inc.

Friedenberg, E. Z. 1965. *The vanishing adolescent.* New York: Dell.

On alienation, the classic reference is still Keniston, K. 1960. *The uncommitted.* New York: Dell. It is of course dated in places; not only was drug use rare at the time, but the alienated youths studied by Keniston were more isolated from one another than they are today. Nevertheless, the book is still amazingly relevant and deserves to be read by anyone seriously interested in modern youth. It contains numerous references.

Though not directed specifically to the problem of alienation, a powerful and accurate commentary on many of the sociological themes mentioned in Chapter III and subsequent chapters is Slater, P. 1970. *The pursuit of loneliness.* Boston: Beacon Press.

Many famous works touch upon various aspects of the origins of alienation. On the question of earlier times vs. recent times:

Riesman, D. 1950. *The lonely crowd.* New Haven: Yale Univ. Press.

Wheelis, A. 1958. *The quest for identity.* New York: Norton.

On primitive societies vs. advanced societies:

Benedict, R. 1954. Continuities and discontinuities in cultural conditioning. In *Readings in child development,* ed. Martin and Stendler. New York: Harcourt Brace and Co.

Mead, M. 1953. *Coming of age in Samoa.* New York: New American Library.

On advanced societies which produce little drug use:

Hsu, F. L. K.; et al. 1963. Culture pattern and adolescent behavior. In *Studies in adolescence,* ed. R. E. Grinder. New York: Macmillan.

Wylie, L. 1966. Youth in France and the United States. In *The challenge of youth,* ed. E. Erikson. Anchor Paperback.

On the distinction between classes:

Bronfenbrenner, U. 1958. Socialization and social class through time and space. In *Readings in social psychology,* 3rd ed., eds. E. E. Maccoby, T. M. Newcomb and E. L. Hartley. New York: Holt, Rinehart, and Winston.

Other references:

Bettelheim, B. 1966. The problem of generations. In *The challenge of youth,* ed. E. Erikson. Anchor Paperback.

Goodman, P. 1960. *Growing up absurd.* New York: Random House.

Keniston, K. 1968-1969. Heads and seekers: Drugs on campus, counter-culture, and American society. *Amer. Scholar* Winter: 97-112.

Parsons, T. 1966. Youth in the context of American society. In *The challenge of youth,* ed. E. Erikson. Anchor Paperback.

Tannenbaum, A. J. 1969. Alienated youth. *J. Social Issues* 25: 1-146.

The word "identity" in this and subsequent chapters is used in the sense of social psychology rather than the more global Eriksonian sense: it refers to a meaningful and lasting involvement with and commitment to an ideology or a group of people; drug users call it, "knowing where you're at." Erikson has himself suggested this might better be called a "pseudo-identity," because it is in itself only an incomplete solution to the overall problem of what he calls identity.

Keniston's extreme group matches Erikson's cases of acute identity confusion; see Erikson, E. 1968. *Identity: Youth and crisis.* New York: Norton. A "pseudo-identity" is rarely the answer for the extreme group; more often the choice is a "negative identity." But as mentioned in the text, most potential users fall in the second echelon of alienation; they are not quite so pessimistic or alienated from their peers that they have given up all hope in searching for a group or ideological identity as a temporary relief from alienation.

Identity: Youth and crisis, like *The uncommitted,* is a "must" for any reader interested in youth. Other psychologically oriented books on youth are:

Blos, P. 1962. *On adolescence.* Glencoe: Free Press. Excellent, but very technical psychoanalytic theory.

Erikson, E. H. 1950. *Childhood and society.* New York: Norton. A great classic.

Freud, A. 1966. *The ego and the mechanisms of defense.* rev. ed., New York: International Universities Press. See chapters 11 and 12.

Another classic similar to *The pursuit of loneliness* (cited above) in its topic is Freud, S. 1961. *Civilization and its discontents,* trans. and ed. J. Strachey. New York: Norton. It is less confusing to the uninitiated reader than most of Freud's works, still relevant, magnificently written.

For Huxley's comment on the enhancement of sentience by hallucinogens, see: Huxley, A. 1954. *The doors of perception,* and

Heaven and Hell. New York: Harper and Row.

For a psychoanalytic commentary related to the fusion experience, see: Brickman, H. R. 1968. The psychedelic "hip scene": Return of the death instinct. *Amer. J. Psychiat.* 125(6): 766-72.

Chapter IV. On the family background of alienated youths, see especially Chapter X in Keniston, K. 1960. *The uncommitted.* New York: Dell, and Chapter III in Slater, P. 1970. *The pursuit of loneliness.* Boston: Beacon Press.

On the status of women in American society and their effect on their children, see:

Friedan, B. 1963. *The feminine mystique.* New York: Norton.

Keniston, E.; and Keniston, K. 1964. An American anachronism: The image of women and work. *Amer. Scholar* 33: 355-75.

Spock, B. 1968. *Baby and child care.* New York: Pocket Books.

Whyte, W. F., Jr. 1962. The wife problem. In *Selected studies in marriage and the family,* eds. R. F. Wench, et al. New York: Holt, Rinehart, and Winston.

For some of the standard descriptions of initiation rites, see Frazer, J. F. 1922. *The golden bough.* 3rd ed., London: Macmillan and Co., Ltd., or Bettelheim, B. 1962. *Symbolic wounds.* New York: Collier, especially pages 113-118, and the many references given in these works.

For Whiting's hypothesis of "brainwashing" the feminine identity, see Burton, R. V.; and Whiting, J. M. 1963. The absent father and cross-sex identity. In *Studies in adolescence,* ed. R. E. Grinder. New York: Macmillan, and especially Whiting, J. M.; Kluckhohn, C.; and Anthony, A. 1958. The function of male initiation ceremonies at puberty. In *Readings in social psychology,* 3rd ed., eds. E. E. Maccoby, T. M. Newcomb, and E. L. Hartley. New York: Holt, Rinehart, and Winston.

One of the most compelling arguments for Whiting's hypothesis (from Whiting, J. M.; Kluckhohn, C.; and Anthony, A. 1958. The function of male initiation ceremonies at puberty. In *Readings in social psychology,* 3rd ed., eds. E. E. Maccoby, T. M. Newcomb, and E. L. Hartley. New

York: Holt, Rinehart, and Winston. 359-370) is a linguistic one: in many societies there is a single word for both "boy" and "woman" and a different word for "man."

On brainwashing in general and the effect of drugs and initiation, see: Sargant, W. 1957. *The battle for the mind.* New York: Doubleday.

A typical discussion of imprinting is Alpert's (pages 52-53) in Alpert, R.; Cohen, S.; and Schiller, L. 1966. *The LSD story.* New York: New American Library. Cohen, on page 92, writes, "I winced at the violence you did to that word 'imprinting' on pages 52-53. This despite the fact that I knew you would. . ." For the proper use of the word, see, Hess, E. H. 1958. "Imprinting" in animals. *Sci. Amer.* March; or Lorenz, K. Z. 1952. *King Solomon's ring.* Thomas Y. Croswell Pub.

Finally, a particularly fascinating article about death and rebirth with particular reference to one of the *gurus* of hallucinogen users, is Halbrook, D. 1968. R. D. Laing and the death-circuit. *Encounter* August.

Chapter V. A fascinating and concise article on the early days of the drug subculture and the old-time hippies is, 1967. A social history of the hippies. *Ramparts* March.

Other descriptions of the early days are:

Staff of Time Magazine. 1967. *The hippies.* New York: Time-Life.

Simmons, J. L.; and Winograd, B. 1967. *It's happening.* Santa Barbara: Marc-Laird Pub.

For a recent description that covers more vividly the elements of anger and withdrawal, read Hoffman, A. 1969. *Woodstock Nation.* New York: Vintage Books.

Also relevant to this chapter is Brickman, H. R. 1968. The psychedelic "hip scene": Return of the death instinct. *Amer. J. Psychiat.* 125(6): 766-72.

For interesting comments about withdrawal and regression to a childhood state, see:

Prince, R.; and Savage, C. 1966. Mystical states and the concept of regression. *Psychedelic Review* 8: 59-75.

Chapter VI. Very little has been written about the sexual activities of drug users, partly because it is practically impossible to study, and partly because it varies so widely between different people. For the general case of homosexuality, see:

Bieber, I.; et. al. 1962. *Homosexuality.* New York: Basic Books. An excellent psychoanalytic study which relates homosexuality to the extreme case of the father-mother-son triangle described in the text.

Sullivan, H. S. 1953. *The interpersonal theory of psychiatry.* eds. H. S. Perry and M. L. Cawel. New York: Norton. Chapter 16 mentions the "buddy" theory of the etiology of homosexuality.

For an idea of the prevalence of homosexuality among drug users, look at the classified "personal" advertisements in most underground newspapers.

Chapter VII. On the use of hallucinogens in psychotherapy by professionals, see:

Abramson, H. A., ed. 1960. *The use of LSD in psychotherapy.* New York: Josiah Macy, Jr. Foundation.

Hoffer, A. 1965. D-lysergic acid diethylamide (LSD): Review of its present status. *Clin. Pharmacol. and Therap.* 6: 183-255. An optimistic viewpoint.

Hoffer, A.; and Osmond, H. 1968. *New hope for alcoholics.* New York: Univ. Books. Promising.

Louria, D.B. 1968. Lysergic acid diethylamide. *N. E. J. Med.* 278(8): 435-38. Pessimistic.

Sarett, M.; et. al. 1966. Reports of wives of alcoholics of effects of LSD-25 treatment of their husbands. *Arch. Gen. Psychiat.* 14: 171-78.

Unger, S.; Kurland, A.; Shaffer, I.; Savage, C.; Wolf, S.; Leihy, R.; McCabe, O.; and Shock, H. 1966. *Psychedelic therapy.* Chicago:

Third Conference on Research in Psychotherapy. Many references are given.

For an attitude closer to that of heavy LSD-users, see the interview with Leary, T. 1967. *Playboy.* September, and Stafford, P. G.; and Golightly, B. H. 1967. *LSD: The problem-solving psychedelic.* New York: Award Books.

There are many books relating psychedelic experiences to Eastern mystical ones, including one of the most eloquent desciiptions of hallucinogen effects ever written, Huxley, A. 1954. *The doors of perception* and *Heaven and Hell.* New York: Harper and Row. See also:

Clark, W. H. 1969. *Chemical ecstasy: Psychedelic drugs and religion.* New York: Sheed and Ward.

Leary, T.; Metzner, R.; and Alpert, R. 1964. *The psychedelic experience.* New York: Univ. Books. A bible for users seeking enlightenment through hallucinogens.

Zaehner, R. C. 1961. *Mysticism, sacred and profane.* New York: Oxford Univ. Press.

See also the original book upon which *The psychedelic experience* is based: Wentz-Evans, W. 1960. *The Tibetan book of the dead.* London: Oxford Univ. Press.

Other books worth reading in order to understand the thought of the older, philosophically-oriented, hallucinogen users:

Roseman, B. 1963. *LSD: The age of the mind.* Hollywood: Wilshire Book Co.

Watts, A. W. 1962. *The joyous cosmology.* New York: Random House, Inc.

A popular account of some interest is Braden, W. 1967. *The private sea: LSD and the search for God.* Chicago: Quadrangle Books.

Finally, the old classic in this field, still very much worth reading, is James, W. 1902. *The varieties of religious experience.* New York: Modern Library.

For some of the philosophies pursued by those who go "beyond" drug use, see:

Laing, R. D. 1967. *The politics of experience.* New York: Ballantine. A book close to the philosophy of many heavy users.

Maharishi Mahesh Yogi. 1966. *The science of being and the art of living.* London: International S.R.M. Publications. A book about Transcendental Meditation and the philosophy behind it.

Maharishi Mahesh Yogi. 1969. *The bhagavad gita: A new translation and commentary.* Baltimore: Penguin.

Ross, N. W., ed. 1969. *The world of Zen.* New York: Random House, Inc. (especially pages 1-36.) A fascinating anthology.

Suzuki, D. T. 1962. *The essentials of Zen Buddhism.* London: Rider and Co. An authoritative treatment.

Watts, A. W. 1957. *The way of Zen.* New York: Pantheon. A good introduction.

Chapter VIII. For an excellent discussion of the career theory of deviance, with special reference to marijuana, see Becker, H. 1963. *Outsiders.* New York: Free Press. Much of my discussion of the drug subculture is based on Becker's theory and terminology.

On the thrill of being outside the law, note page 164 in Sullivan, H. S. 1953. *Conceptions of modern psychiatry.* New York: Norton.

Of numerous studies on reference groups and attitude change, two classics are Asch, S. E. 1965. Effects of group pressure upon the modification of and distortion of judgements. In *Basic studies in social psychology,* eds. H. Proshansky and B. Seidenberg. New York: Holt, Rinehart, and Winston, or 1958. In *Readings in social psychology,* eds. E. Maccoby, T. Newcomb, and E. Hartley. New York: Holt; and Newcomb, T. 1965. Attitude development as a function of reference groups. In *Basic studies in social psychology,* eds. H. Proshansky and B. Seidenberg. New York: Holt, Rinehart, and Winston, or 1958. In *Readings in social psychology,* eds. E. Maccoby, T. Newcomb, and E. Hartley. New York: Holt.

On "cognitive dissonance," see Festinger, L.; and Aronson, E. 1960. The arousal and reduction of dissonance in social contexts. In *Group dynamics,* 2nd ed., eds. D. Cartwright and A. Zander. New York: Row and Peterson: 214-32.

The idea that societies encourage deviance is discussed on pages 9-22 by Erikson, K. T. 1964. Notes on the sociology of deviance. In *The other side,* ed. H. S. Becker. New York: Free Press. *The other side* contains several other interesting articles about deviance.

For further information on drug subcultures, see:

Becker, H. S. 1967. History, culture and subjective experience: An exploration of the social bases of drug-induced experiences. *J. of Health and Behavior* 8(3): 163-76.

Blum, R. H.; et al. 1970. *Society and drugs.* San Francisco: Jossey-Bass, Inc. The companion volume to *Students and drugs,* already cited.

Horman, R. E.; and Fox, A. M. 1970. *Drug awareness.* New York: Avon Books.

Kaufman, J.; Allen, J.; and West, L. J. 1969. Runaways, hippies and marihuana. *Amer. J. Psychiat.* 126: 717-20.

On the role of the media in the drug subculture, see: Barber, B. 1967. *Drugs and society.* New York: Russell Sage Foundation.

Chapter IX. A superb general reference on pharmacology, including material about all of the drug categories discussed in the text, is Goodman, L. S.; and Gilman, A. 1970. *The pharmacological basis of therapeutics.* 4th ed., New York: Macmillan.

Bibliographic material on marijuana:

Kalant, O. J. 1968. *An interim guide to the cannabis (marijuana) literature.* Toronto: Addiction Research Foundation. An excellent critical bibliography of 20 works.

Moore, L. A., Jr. 1968. *Marihuana (cannabis) bibliography.* Los Angeles: Bruin Humanist Forum. Exhaustive but without critical commentary.

Murphy, H. B. M. 1966. The cannabis habit: A review of recent psychiatric literature. *U. N. Bull. on Narcotics* 15(1): 15-23, 103. Also in 1966. *Addictions* 13(1): 3-26. A good review with 58 references. Highly recommended.

General discussions of marijuana:

Andrews, G.; and Vinkenoog, S., eds. 1967. *The book of grass.* New York: Grove Press. Many interesting selections.

Bloomquist, E. R. 1968. *Marijuana.* Beverly Hills: Glencoe Press. A well balanced presentation.

Goode, E., ed. 1969. *Marijuana.* New York: Atherton Press. Also well balanced.

Grinspoon, L. 1971. *Marihuana reconsidered.* Cambridge: Harvard Univ. Press. An incisive and accurate commentary; probably the best single book available on the assets and liabilities of marihuana.

McGlothlin, W. H.; and West, L. J. 1968. The marijuana problem: An overview. *Amer. J. Psychiat.* 125: 370-78.

Mayor's Committee on Marijuana. 1944. *The marijuana problem in the City of New York.* Lancaster, Penn.: Jacques Cattell Press. Though old, this is still very accurate and relevant.

Simmons, J. L. 1967. *Marijuana, myths and realities.* Hollywood: Brandon House. Good for the inexperienced reader.

Solomon, D. 1960. *The marijuana papers.* Indianapolis: Bobbs-Merrill Co. An excellent and thorough coverage.

Two fiery condemnations of marijuana:

Anslinger, H. J. 1953. *The traffic in narcotics.* New York: Funk and Wagnalls.

St. Charles, A. J. 1952. *The narcotics menace.* Los Angeles: Bosden.

Two classic studies on the chemistry of marijuana and hashish:

Isbell, H.; Gorodetzsky, C. W.; Jasinski, D.; Claussen, U.; Speulak, F.; and Korte, R. 1967. Effects of $(-)\Delta^9$-Trans-tetrahydrocannabinol in man. *Psychopharmacologia 11: 184-88.*

Wolstenhalme, G. E. W.; and Knight, J., eds. 1965. *Hashish: Its chemistry and pharmacology.* (CIBA Symposium). Boston: Little,

Brown.

Laboratory studies of the effects of marijuana in man:

Allentuck, S.; and Bowman, K. M. 1942. The psychiatric aspects of marijuana intoxication. *Amer. J. Psychiat.* 99: 248.

Clark, L. D.; and Nakashima, E. N. 1968. Experimental studies of marihuana. *Amer. J. Psychiat.* 125: 379-84.

Silar, J. F.; Sheep, W. L.; Bates, L. B.; Clark, G. F.; Cook, G. W.; and Smith, W. A. 1933. Marihuana smoking in Panama. *Mil. Surg.* 73: 269.

Weil, A. T.; Zinberg, N. E.; and Nelson, J. M. 1968. Clinical and psychological effects of marihuana in man. *Science* 162: 1234-42.

Weil, A. T.; Zinberg, N. E.; and Nelson, J. M. 1969. Acute effects of marihuana on speech. *Nature* May: 222.

On the effects of long-term use of marijuana and hashish in foreign countries:

Benabed, A. 1957. Psycho-pathological aspects of the cannabis situation in Morrocco: Statistical data for 1956. *Bull. on Narcotics* 9: 1-16.

Chopra, I. C.; and Chopra, R. N. 1960. The use of cannabis drugs in India. *U. N. Bull. on Narcotics* 9(1): 4-29.

Sovief, M. I. 1967. Hashish consumption in Egypt with special reference to psychosocial aspects. *Bull. on Narcotics* 19: 1-12.

Excellent general texts on the pharmacology of the hallucinogens are the following:

Aaronson, B.; and Osmond, H., eds. 1970. *Psychedelics.* Garden City, N.Y.: Doubleday, Anchor. Excellent bibliography.

Hoffer, A.; and Osmond, H. 1967. *The hallucinogens.* New York: Free Press. More technical than *Psychedelics,* cited above.

McGlothlin, W. H. 1965. Hallucinogenic drugs: A perspective with special reference to peyote and cannabis. Washington: U.S. Government Printing Office. Reprinted in *Psychedelic Review*

1965(6): 16-57. Shorter and well-presented.

Probably the best description of the subjective effects of LSD is Masters, R. E. L.; and Houston, J. 1967. *The varieties of psychedelic experiences.* New York: Delta.

A popular work, *The LSD story,* (cited above) is interesting for its contrasting viewpoints.

These other excellent general works on LSD and its use are:

Blum, R.; et al. 1964. *Utopiates: The use and users of LSD–25.* New York: Atherton. Especially interesting material on the history of LSD use in U.S.A.

Debold, R. C.; and Leaf, R. C. 1967. *LSD, man and society.* Middletown, Conn.: Wesleyan Univ. Press. Moderately technical.

Solomon, D. 1964. *LSD: The consciousness-expanding drug.* New York: G. P. Putnam's Sons. Many fascinating essays by famous contributors.

Studies on the chromosomal effects of LSD:

Positive findings:

Cohen, M. M., et al. 1967. *In vivo* and *in vitro* chromosomal damage induced by LSD–25. *N. E. J. Med.* 277: 1045-49.

Irwin, S.; and Egozcue, J. 1967. Chromosomal abnormalities in leukocytes from LSD users. *Science* 157: 313-15.

Negative findings:

Bender, Y. L.; and Siva Sankar, P. V. 1968. Chromosome damage not found in leukocytes of children treated with LSD–25. *Science* 159: 749.

Judd, L. L.; Brandkamp, W. W.; and McGlothlin, W. H. 1970. Comparison of the chromosomal patterns obtained from groups of continued users, former users, and non-users of LSD–25. *Amer. J. Psychiat.* 12b: 626-35.

Loughman, W. D.; et al. 1967. Leukocytes of humans exposed to lysergic acid diethylamide: Lack of chromosomal damage.

Science 158: 508-10.

Sparkes, R. S.; et al. 1968. Chromosomal effect *in vivo* of exposure to lysergic acid diethylamide. *Science* 160: 1343.

The famous *in vitro* study by Cohen, M. M.; et al. 1967. Chromosomal damage in human leukocytes induced by lysergic acid diethylamide. *Science* 155: 1417-19, also included findings of damage in a single subject. This study should best be ignored; it exposed cells to concentrations of LSD ranging from 10 times to 1,000,000 the normal concentration after a 100 μgm dose in man. See the excellent criticisms of this study in Loughman, W. D.; et al. 1967. Leukocytes of humans exposed to lysergic acid diethylamide: Lack of chromosomal damage. *Science* 158: 508-10. In fact, Loughman, et al. demonstrate that the Cohen *in vitro* study supports their negative findings.

Published descriptions of LSD "flashbacks" include:

Frosch, W. A.; et al. 1965. Untoward reactions to LSD resulting in hospitalization. *N. E. J. Med.* 273: 1235-39.

Ungeleider, J. T.; and Fisher, D. D. 1966. LSD: Fact and fantasy. *Progr. Archit.* 83: 18-20.

On prolonged LSD-after effects, see the two cited above and the following:

Aaronson, B.; and Osmond, H., eds. 1970. *Psychedelics.* Garden City, N.Y.: Doubleday, Anchor.

Barron, S. P.; Lowinger, P.; and Evner, E. 1970. A clinical examination of chronic LSD use in the community. *Compr. Psychiat.* 11: 69-79.

Cohen, S.; and Ditman, K. S. 1963. Prolonged adverse reactions to lysergic acid diethylamide. *Arch. Gen. Psychiat.* 8(5): 475-80.

Debold, R. C.; and Leaf, R. C. 1967. *LSD, man and society.* Middletown, Conn.: Wesleyan Univ. Press.

Ditman, K. S.; et al. 1968. Harmful aspects of the LSD experience. *J. Nerv. Ment. Dis.* 145: 464-71.

Fink, M.; et al. 1966. Prolonged adverse reactions to LSD in psychotic subjects. *Arch. Gen. Psychiat.* 15: 450-54.

Hoffer, A.; and Osmond, H. 1967. *The hallucinogens.* New York: Free Press.

Klever, H. D. 1967. Prolonged adverse reactions from unsupervised use of hallucinogenic drugs. *J. Nerv. Ment. Dis.* 144: 308-19.

Louria, D. B. 1968. *The drug scene.* New York: McGraw-Hill. The scare-story approach.

McGlothlin, W. H.; et al. 1967. Long-lasting effects of LSD in normals. *Arch. Gen. Psychiat.* 17: 521-32.

Milbauer, B.; and Leinwald, G., eds. 1970. *Drugs.* Even less desirable than Louria, above.

Rosenthal, S. H. 1964. Persistent hallucinosis following repeated administration of hallucinogen drugs. *Amer. J. Psychiat.* 121: 238-44.

Ungeleider, J. T.; et al. 1968. A statistical survey of adverse reactions to LSD in Los Angeles County. *Amer. J. Psychiat.* 125: 352.

In a class by itself is Blacker, K. H.; Jones, R. T.; Stone, G. C.; and Pfeffervaum, D. 1968. Chronic users of LSD: The "acidheads." *Amer. J. Psychiat.* 125: 341-51. A description of heavy LSD-users which agrees almost perfectly with my experiences.

On the pharmacology, subjective effects, and cultural aspects of other specific hallucinogens:

Mescaline and Peyote:

Klüver, H. 1966. *Mescal and mechanisms of hallucinations.* Chicago: Univ. of Chicago Press.

La Barre, W. 1964. *The Peyote cult* Hamden: The Shoestring Press.

On STP (DOM), DOET, and TMA, MDA, MMDA, and other substituted amphetamines:

Hollister, L. E. 1969. An hallucinogenic amphetamine (DOM) in man. *Psychopharmacologia* 14: 62-73.

Naranjo, D.; Shulgin, A. T.; and Sargent, I. 1967. Evaluation of 3,4-methylenedioxyamphetamine (MDA) as an adjunct to psychotherapy. *Med. Pharmacol. Exp.* 17: 359-64.

Shulgin, A. T.; Bunnell, S.; and Sargent, T. 1961. The psychotomimetic properties of 3,4,5-trimethoxyamphetamine. *Nature* 189: 1011-12. On TMA.

Shulgin, A. T. 1964. 3-methoxy-4,5-methylenedioxyamphetamine, a new psychotomimetic agent. *Nature* 201: 1120-21. On MMDA.

Snyder, S. H.; et al. 1967. 2,5-dimethoxy-4-methyl-amphetamine (STP): A new hallucinogenic drug. *Science* 158: 669-70.

Snyder, S. H.; et al. 1968. DOM (STP), a new hallucinogenic drug, and DOET: Effects in normal subjects. *Amer. J. Psychiat.* 357-364.

On hallucinogens of plant origin, see:

Efron, D. H., ed. 1967. *Ethnopharmacologic search for psychoactive drugs.* [Public Health Service Publication No. 1645]. Washington, D.C., U.S. Dept. of Health, Education, and Welfare: U.S. Government Printing Office.

Schultes, R. E. 1969, 1970. The plant kingdom and hallucinogens. *Bull. Narcotics* [Part I] 21(3): 3-16. [Part II] 21(4): 15-27. [Part III] 22(1): 25-53.

Schultes, R. E. 1969. Hallucinogens of plant origin. *Science* 163: 245-254.

Highly recommended for their description of hallucinogens in primitive cultures:

Aberle, D. F. 1966. *The peyote religion among the Navaho.* Chicago: Aldine.

Castaneda, C. 1969. *The teachings of Don Juan: A Yaqui way of knowledge.* New York: Ballantine Books. A beautiful first-person account.

Pope, H. 1969. Tabernanthe iboga: an African narcotic of social importance. *J. Econ. Bot.* 23(2): 174-84.

Slotkin, J. 1956. *The peyote religion.* Glencoe: Free Press.

Chapter X. Good general works on amphetamines are:

Kalant, O. J. 1966. *The amphetamines: Toxicity and addiction.* Toronto: Univ. of Toronto Press.

Leake, C. D. 1958. *The amphetamines: Their actions and uses.* Springfield, Ill.: Thomas. Includes a good description of the "crash".

For the specific case of amphetamine psychosis, see:

Connell, P. H. 1958. *Amphetamine psychosis.* London: Chapman and Hall, Ltd.

More timely information may be found in Smith, D. E., ed. 1969. Speed kills: A review of amphetamine drug abuse. *J. Psychedel. Drugs* 2. This also includes a good deal of information about the hallucinogenic amphetamine derivatives, TMA, MDA, DOM, MMDA, etc. All of the above works include extensive bibliographies which the reader may consult for further information.

On cocaine, see:

Adriani, J. 1960. The clinical pharmacology of local anesthetics. *Clin. Pharmac. Ther.* 1: 645-73.

Bejerot, N. 1970. A comparison of the effects of cocaine and synthetic central stimulants. *Brit. J. Addict.* 65: 35-37.

Chapter XI. Two excellent multidisciplinary works about opiate use are:

Chein, I.; Gerard, D. L.; Lee, R. S.; and Rosenfeld, E; with the collaboration of D. M. Wilner). 1964. *The road to H: Narcotics, Delinquency, and social policy.* New York: Basic Books. Primarily psychological in orientation.

Wilner, D.; and Kassebaum, G., eds. 1965. *Narcotics.* New York: McGraw-Hill. Excellent, but neglects cultural and subcultural aspects of use.

A superb first-person account of the heroin world, giving a good idea of the organization and jargon of the subculture is, Burroughs, W. S. 1953. *Junkie.* New York: Ace.

On the masculinity of heroin use, see Finestone, H. Cats, kids, and color. In *The Other Side,* already cited.

A fascinating account of life in Harlem is Brown, C. 1965. *Manchild in the promised land.* New York: Signet. Though not about the drug users discussed in this book, it contains a personal description of a typical frightening first experience (pages 110-111), and conjectures about heroin use as an identity.

For general information of the pharmacology of opiates, see:

Reynolds, A. K.; and Randall, L. O. 1957. *Morphine and allied drugs.* Toronto: Univ. of Toronto Press.

An interesting account of organized narcotic dealing is Moscow, A. 1968. *Merchants of heroin.* New York: Dial Press.

On the pharmacology of addiction, see especially Esbell, H.; and Fraser, H. F. 1950. Addiction to analgesics and barbiturates. *Pharmac. Rev.* 2: 355-97.

On the work of Synanon, see:

Austin, B. L. 1970. *Sad nun at synanon.* New York: Holt, Rinehart, and Winston.

Yablonsky, L. 1965. *The tunnel back: Synanon.* New York: Macmillan.

Good reviews of other "downs" include:

Adams, E. 1958. Barbiturates. *Sci. Amer.* 198: 60-64.

Domino, E. F. 1962. Human pharmacology of tranquilizing drugs. *Clin. Pharmac. Ther.* 3: 599-664.

References not already recommended:

Adler, N. 1969. The antinomian personality. *Psychiatry* 31: 325. This article suggests that the modern street subculture is a recent manifestation of a type that has occurred in conditions of political strain for centuries.

Allen, J. R.; and West, L. J. 1968. Flight from violence: Hippies and the green rebellion. *Amer. J. Psychiat.* 125: 364-70. One of the handful of professional articles based on a good deal of direct observation.

Ebin, D. 1965. *The drug experience.* New York: Grove Press. An interesting anthology of first-person accounts.

Gitchoff, G. T. 1969. *Kids, cops, and kilos: A study of contemporary suburban youth.* San Diego: Malter-Westerfield. Drugs in suburbia.

Harris, R. T.; McIsaac, W. M.; and Schuster, C. R. 1970. *Drug dependence.* Austin: Univ. of Texas Press. A broad treatment of many aspects of drug use.

Sarbin, R. R. 1969. On the distinction between social roles and social types, with special references to the hippies. *Amer. J. Psychiat.* 125: 1024.

Wolfe, T. 1968. *The electric kool-aid acid test.* New York: Farrar, Straus, and Giroux. Interesting historically.

The following, though popular, are not strongly recommended:

Fort, J. 1969. *The pleasure seekers.* New York: Grove Press.

Gustaitis, R. 1969. *Turning on.* New York: Signet Books.

Stearn, J. 1969. *The Seekers: Drugs and the new generation.* New York: Doubleday.